BROTHERS!

CALLING MEN INTO VITAL RELATIONSHIPS

A Small Group Discussion Guide

GEOFF GORSUCH
with DAN SCHAFFER

PROMISE
K E E P E R S

NAVPRESS
BRINGING TRUTH TO LIFE
NavPress Publishing Group
P.O. Box 35001, Colorado Springs, Colorado 80935

The Navigators is an international Christian organization.
Jesus Christ gave His followers the Great Commission to go
and make disciples (Matthew 28:19). The aim of The
Navigators is to help fulfill that commission by multiplying
laborers for Christ in every nation.

NavPress is the publishing ministry of The Navigators.
NavPress publications are tools to help Christians grow.
Although publications alone cannot make disciples or
change lives, they can help believers learn biblical discipleship, and apply what they learn to their lives and ministries.

Second printing, 1994

Unless otherwise identified, all Scripture quotations in this
publication are taken from the *HOLY BIBLE: NEW INTER-
NATIONAL VERSION* ® (NIV®). Copyright ©1973, 1978,
1984 by International Bible Society. Used by permission of
Zondervan Publishing House. All rights reserved. Another
version used is the *King James Version*(KJV).

Printed in the United States of America

5 6 7 8 9 10 11 12 13 14 15 16 17/99 98 97 96 95

FOR A FREE CATALOG OF
NAVPRESS BOOKS & BIBLE STUDIES,
CALL 1-800-366-7788 (USA)
or 1-416-499-4615 (CANADA)

Contents

Foreword...5

Chapter 1
    A New Look at Baseball...9

Chapter 2
    Heading for First..21

Chapter 3
    Sliding into Second..33

Chapter 4
    Rounding Third..45

Chapter 5
    Coming Home 55

Chapter 6
    The Coach: A Servant-Leader 63

Chapter 7
    Breaking Into the Game: The Reconciliation Process 71

Chapter 8
    The Equipment Closet: Troubleshooting 83

Appendix 1
    "One Another" Bible Study..91

Appendix 2
    Accountability Questions for Men's Small Groups.................95

Appendix 3
    The Joy of DSI: Discovery, Sharing, and Interceding 97

Appendix 4
    Confusion and Isolation in the American Male....................101

Appendix 5
    "The Baselines"...105

Appendix 6
    More on Listening Skills. 107

Bibliography 109

Foreword

We at Promise Keepers are seeing a revival in the hearts of men across the country. As a result, we are being asked for assistance in developing small groups which will help men grow to maturity in Christ. In this age of individualism, men are finally beginning to realize the importance of having brothers who will support, encourage, and hold one another accountable to a Christian model of manhood. As one of our promises states: "A Promise Keeper is committed to pursue vital relationships with a few other men, understanding that he needs brothers to help him keep his promises."

In order to help men become the brothers Christ intended them to be, Promise Keepers is proud to present *Brothers! Calling Men Into Vital Relationships*. To offer this resource to you, we called upon Mr. Geoff Gorsuch of The Navigators and Mr. Dan Schaffer of our own Promise Keepers staff to consolidate their years of experience in men's ministry into this small but very informative book. Within these pages, therefore, you will find not only the inspiration but also the practical tools you will need to develop your own small group of brothers! I heartily recommend it to you along with my personal prayer that God will richly reward your efforts.

—E. Glenn Wagner, Ph.D.
Vice President of National Ministries,
Promise Keepers

Acknowledgments

Both Dan and I are very thankful for the prayer and effort of those who have patiently worked with us on this project. In that light, we'd like to mention Glenn Wagner, Randy Phillips, and Pete Richardson of the Promise Keepers staff who helped us determine the basic direction of the book. We would also like to thank Mr. Eric Swanson of Campus Crusade for Christ whose timely counsel on the content and tone of the book helped us bring the project to completion. Also, we would like to mention Mrs. Meg Watson, an accomplished grammarian, who patiently edited all the rewrites to help us say it better.

Most importantly, however, we wish to thank our wives, Diane and Jan, for their encouragement along the way. We couldn't have done it without them.

—Geoff Gorsuch

Chapter 1

A New Look at Baseball

"Faith, hope, and love," Larry said, "that's the way I see it, guys. It all boils down to faith, hope, and love." Then he reached for his Bible and turned to the book of Romans, chapter five. "Paul said all that comes our way down here is to challenge us to grow in one of these three vital areas: faith in God, love for our fellow man, and hope in the future—God's future for us.

"If we grow, we'll take on some of the nature of Christ Himself. That's the reward: Christlikeness! But it's a struggle—a struggle we can't escape." He added, "But we certainly can help each other with it—what do you think?"

As Larry continued to relate these cardinal virtues of Scripture to the discussion already in progress, the others gradually joined in. With their coffee in one hand and their Bibles in the other, their biweekly men's meeting had begun.

Though Larry was prepared to lead the discussion, each man had studied the text enough to present his own ideas. Everyone knew that by the end of the evening, however, his impressions would be altered by what his friends had shared. That's why they came; that's what they wanted. In his own unique way, each man had learned that he could not live out his Christian life alone.

They'd tried. Oh! How they'd tried. But their successes were mixed with stories about children and drugs, problems with debt, struggling marriages and divorce. They'd learned that "life happens"! However, what they'd experienced with this group of men when these events did happen had changed their lives. In fact, they had learned so much about life, themselves, and God that now they could honestly say, "The pain has been worth it!"

Since they knew each other so well, everyone felt the freedom to be himself. So, to no one's surprise, the attorney in the group volunteered to present his case first. As he spoke, there were numerous head nods, some note-taking and the inevitable questions which sought understanding, not confrontation. Each took a turn to share his discoveries about life in general and his life in particular. There was no shame, no apologies; just a comfortable conversation with the guys.

Later, however, while everyone was examining Abraham's faith, Jerry, the finish carpenter in the group, pointed out with great concern that Abraham often seemed to lack faith. This comment produced a vigorous discussion. However, though they were clearly enjoying the dialogue, that was not the only reason they came.

Toward the end of the evening, Jerry hesitantly brought up for a second time Abraham's apparent abandonment of his wife. This was clearly an "act of cowardice" in his opinion. When some of the others rose to Abraham's defense, the carpenter angrily replied, "But why does God commend a person like Abraham when he did that to his wife?"

After an uncomfortable silence, Larry sensitively began to bring up the subject of Jerry's recent divorce.

"Do you feel like you treated your wife better than Abraham treated his?"

"I treated her like a queen," Jerry said.

"Do you feel like you deserved a successful marriage because you treated your wife so well?"

"Well," Jerry paused, "I sure didn't deserve a divorce!"

Then Larry asked the question that was on everyone's minds: "Are you mad at God because your wife left you?"

"It just seems," Jerry hesitated, "that God could have changed her heart. I tried to be faithful to her and to God. My conscience is clear." Shaking his head, Jerry sadly concluded, "I just don't get it." Fighting back the tears, he buried his head in his hands and again mumbled, "I just don't get it."

Neither did they, but they'd been praying for Jerry for months, and the profound silence that followed Jerry's anger revealed God's presence. Their prayers had been answered.

After a respectful pause, Larry asked the group, "Well, guys, what do you think? Can God really be trusted . . . even when it hurts? Can we grow in Christlikeness, even when the pain is so great that we want to run away?"

The answer was, "Yes!" Because of their relationships, the men felt free to rally to their brother in need. What's more important, Jerry felt free to let them. He accepted their encouragement and their loving challenges to "hang in there." The sensitivity with which Larry and the others chose their words clearly demonstrated Christ's love.

Finally, Jerry stopped trying to justify himself and broke down in tears. Yes, real men cry. Jesus did! The pain and disappointment that he had been carrying for months had finally caught up to him. However, they all understood. In his own way each one had been there; and because they had, Jerry could trust them. As he admitted his failure, there was no condemnation on anyone's lips, no judgment—just "truth spoken in love."

Praying with him, they helped Jerry open up again to God. As his deep feelings of betrayal departed, this strong man finally choked out a prayer of confession for his anger toward God. As Larry closed their evening together, he prayed that they'd continue to be honest with God and one another no matter what the cost.

Lingering at the door, each hesitated to break the mood by leaving, for they had gotten what they really came for—a divine encounter! They had grown in their awareness of God and the ministry of the Holy Spirit in their daily lives, and they were very thankful.

As they parted company, a couple of the guys decided to take Jerry out for a late dinner. It had been months since he'd done more than just pick at his food, and suddenly he'd gotten his appetite back. They laughed as they walked away, wondering just how much the bill would be and who would pay!

While Larry cleaned up, he thought of the Apostle Paul's longing to "be encouraged together with you . . . each of us by the other's faith." What had been so special about the evening, he thought, was its authenticity. It had been real, so real! Real men had faced real life issues together and won! He'd been waiting a long time for this. As he thought about how to tap the full potential of the group, he wondered what lay ahead for them as they continued to face life together.

❖

We wrote this book for men like Jerry, Larry—and you. Men who are no longer kidding themselves. Men who have learned that being a loner doesn't cut it. Men who are convinced that the key to their maturity in Christ is to find men of like heart and to grow—to struggle!—with them.

Being a mature man has never been easy. But the Bible teaches us that there are spiritual resources available to help us face the challenge. God has given us His Spirit, His Word, and one another so that we don't have to do the job alone. In that light, we must decide: Will we still insist on going it alone or will we become part of a group of men and assume our role as a brother in Christ?

Why Brothers?
The cross is not the end of a search; it is the beginning of an adventure! To come to belief in God through the cross of Jesus Christ is only an introduction to all that men were intended to be. As the Apostle Paul said:

> And we know that in all things God works for the good of those who love him, who have been *called* according to his purpose ... to be conformed to the likeness of his Son, that he might be the firstborn among many brothers. (Romans 8:28-29, italics added)

This passage clearly teaches that not only were we touched to become like "His Son," but that God will use "all things" that happen to and through our lives for that "purpose." The key to our growth, however, is how we will respond to God's call.

THE PURPOSE OF GOD'S CALL

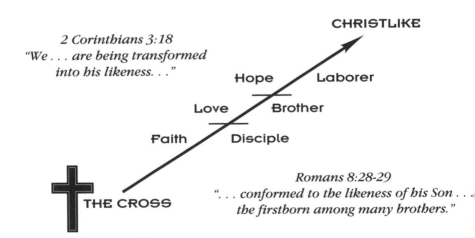

12

Faith

Contrary to popular belief, faith is a verb. That is, it acts! Faith courageously moves into the unknown based upon what is hoped for in the future (Hebrews 11:1). Faith takes risks. Faith invests. However, to learn to invest our lives in that which is worthy, a man must start at the cross and become Christ's disciple. That is where our response begins. A disciple is a learner! He's an apprentice who follows his master by faith.

However, in the book of Acts, the word *disciple* is gradually replaced by another word. This word appears over two hundred times in the New Testament and represents the next phase of our commitment to Christ. The word is *brother*. It is as brothers that the full intent of Christ's life and mission to the world is to be lived out.

What is a Brother?

Brothers are the sons of a common father. If you are a child of God and I am a child of God, it is undeniable that we are brothers. The same royal blood has been shed for us. We are heirs of a common spiritual inheritance, so as brothers we should be available for one another. Brothers stand in defense of one another. Brothers fight for each other and at times may even die for each other. In a manly way, they learn to love "one another."

The "One Anothers"

According to the New Testament, the way Christ's love is manifested is by practicing the "one anothers." Therefore, as brothers we should "honor one another." We should "serve one another." We should "encourage one another." We should even "bear one another's burdens" as we "pray for one another." And the list goes on.

In fact, there are over fifty commands relating to "one another" in the New Testament. (See the Bible study on the "one anothers" in appendix 1.) All of these commands, however, can be summed up under three major headings: to *accept, encourage,* and *exhort* "one another." The way these concepts build upon each other is the dynamic of brotherly love and the foundation of effective men's small groups.

Acceptance

"Accept one another, then, just as Christ accepted you" (Romans 15:7). How did Christ accept us? Unconditionally. He's more interested in where we want to go than in where we've been. Therefore, our attitude should be the same.

The first job of men's small groups is to learn complete accept-ance: no judgment, no "I told you so" or "you should have known better." No hidden agendas! I'm not out to change you and you're not out to change me. If you and I feel that we have to put on a spiritual mask in order to be part of a small group, we won't stick around very long. Complete acceptance, however, will create a safe place where men can really be themselves.

Encouragement

"Therefore, encourage one another and build each other up" (1 Thessalonians 5:11). The word *encourage* comes from the same word as one of the names of the Holy Spirit. It is a word meaning "called alongside to help." To encourage one another, then, is to be vitally involved in what the Spirit is doing in the lives of our brothers in Christ. Either verbally or through our actions, we can affirm God's view of our brothers. In doing so, we move from accepting them to helping them in some tangible way. Encouragement is taking an active role in a brother's life.

Exhortation

"Let the word of Christ dwell in you richly as you teach and admon-ish one another with all wisdom" (Colossians 3:16-17). The Apostle Paul says that "speaking the truth in love" we are to grow in Christ (Ephesians 4:15). How do we grow spiritually? How do we become the men God wants us to be? *Growth comes from truth shared through meaningful relationships*. Through "teaching" we learn how God wants us to live. "Admonishing" is helping each other apply those truths, even when it is difficult. We all fall short, but we all must keep trying! The group can become God's means of loving correction to help us apply the truth to our lives. This is exhortation as God intended it to be—brothers lovingly prodding one another to do their best.

Hope

In spite of what we have seen and heard in our highly individual-istic culture, it is clear that Christ never wanted His disciples to live out their Christian lives alone. Where the brothers are accept-ing, encouraging, and exhorting one another to full maturity in

Christ, there is love, and that love is the hope of the world!

As people see the love of the brothers in action, they will see hope for their own lives and somewhere to turn for real help. This is what Jesus meant when He said the world would know we are His if we love one another (John 13:34-35). Love kindles hope, and as a mature brother, a man can become a laborer in God's Kingdom as he takes that hope to his family, his friends and, ultimately, to the world.

The Obstacles to Brotherhood

However, in spite of this clear biblical mandate to "love one another," our research indicates that most Christian men struggle profoundly with their relationships. Many would like to have friends on whom they could count: brothers! Yet, in spite of these desires, we have learned that most adult American males are relatively friendless.

In response to this phenomenon, Pat Morely, in his book *The Man in the Mirror*, offers us a list of questions that are very helpful in defining the quality of our man-to-man relationships. Here are just a few:

◆ When things go badly, whom do you talk to?
◆ Who can you be totally honest with?
◆ Who is your sounding board?
◆ Who would you take advice from?
◆ When you fail, who will stand by you?
◆ Who do you face life's struggles with?
◆ Who is your confidant?
◆ Who holds you accountable?

Are there some men in your life you can really count on? Where do you go when "life happens"? Do you have friends like Larry, men who know you well enough to be brothers? If not, then you may be living in relative isolation, caught in relational patterns that allow you to function but not to grow in Christ.

We have discovered that there are two major reasons why this quality is often lacking in male relational patterns here in North America. The first one is that men, in general, are more prone to be loners than women are. Many researchers have noted that this just seems to be a part of the male nature. (This concept will be more fully developed in chapter 2.) Second, in North America, there are cultural forces that push that loner in us all to extremes (For more on the subject of male pattern isolation, please refer to appendix 4.)

In light of these tendencies, therefore, we would like to propose the following model—the baseball diamond— for your guidance and encouragement as you bring loners together to become brothers.

Spring Training

Most professional teams go to Florida or Arizona in the spring to get ready for the season. We'd like to suggest that a men's group also needs time to get ready to play. When you have developed a lineup of men who want to face life together as brothers, use this book for a period of spring training to prepare the team for the actual season. Use this book as an eight-session guide to beginning a men's group. Ask participants to read the chapter before they come to each session so they will be prepared to discuss the questions at the end of each chapter. As you discuss the rules of the game and their biblical basis, each player will have time to decide whether or not he's ready to play.

Training is vital to prepare each man to take the risks necessary to form a team of brothers. In this way, those who feel ready will have a better idea of what to expect. For those who hesitate because of the risks involved, we can only remind them that Christ, our model of manhood, chose to live out His life and ministry in the context of a small group of men. If He felt He needed brothers, how much more do we?

Because relationships usually develop slowly with men, we'll need to have time and coaching to play this game. We're all old enough to know that we have time for what we really want to do. So, if becoming a brother is important, we'll make the time. Secondly, every team needs a coach, or better yet, a player-coach who can help the players move from base to base successfully. Spring Training should reveal who's best qualified to fulfill that role.

The Bases

The process of building vital relationships among men can be likened to a baseball diamond in that there are four phases of development. The process starts as we step up to the plate with

THE RELATIONAL DIAMOND

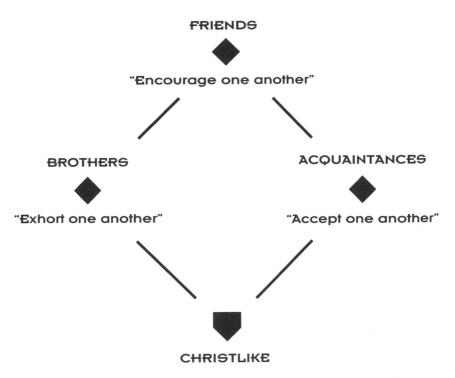

FRIENDS

"Encourage one another"

BROTHERS

"Exhort one another"

ACQUAINTANCES

"Accept one another"

CHRISTLIKE

the desire and the determination to become more like Christ. Then the men become acquainted with each other at first base. At second base, the relationships progress to the level of friendship. From there, we round third base and head toward home plate as communication and commitment to one another deepen. Thus, we become the brothers Christ intends us to be.

As you can see in the diagram, each base on our relational diamond corresponds to a biblical command relating to the "one anothers" which we previously discussed. At first base we learn to "accept one another" and explore the potential of the relationships. At second base, we develop our friendships as we "encourage and build up one another." At third base, after much time and coaching, we should feel free to "exhort one another" as we face life's challenges together. At this point we're brothers, vitally interested in helping each other reach home plate—growth in Christlikeness.

Each phase in and of itself is good and serves its purpose to keep us in the game. However, all acquaintances and friends do not have to become brothers. In fact, our limited emotional capacity will not permit it. But if we will keep stepping up to the plate and taking a few swings—risks!—we can become the brothers of a few. And that's what the game is all about. So, "Let's play ball!"

Heading for First

Though activities do not guarantee solid relationships, men seem to need activities more than women do to get to know one another better. Men will enter more easily into the task of trust building in the context of shared experiences. These activities may vary from sporting events to cultural events depending upon the tastes of the men involved. But their goal is always the same—to help the men "accept one another" in Christ.

Light, cliché-level conversation should characterize this phase. That's all right as long as we're willing to listen to each other. As the relationships progress, the players can explore options and arrive at a form of activity and communication which seems to meet their needs. The group's purpose, what it wants to do and why, should be settled as soon as possible. Though this may not be decided until the group has been meeting for a while, in most cases the group's purpose is well established by the time it approaches second.

Sliding into Second

Sliding implies friction!

When men gather, there will be a need to adjust expectations for the group in an honest but respectful way. The conversation must pass from the cliché level to the level of ideas and opinions. This progression requires skill in leading discussions and resolving conflicts.

When men fight fair, that is, when they are encouraged to fully express themselves on men's issues, they develop a bond of trust with each other. This trust produces communication that is based on mutual respect. Without it, the group will dissolve.

Because of the conflict, however, men will be tempted to steal second and not allow the time necessary to work through the relational patterns. In this game, however, there is no stealing because men need time to feel comfortable with each other.

18

Rounding Third

Too many groups approach third base and then turn right! In other words, they never get to exhortation. They never get to covenants and accountability. They never enter into the struggle for moral excellence together. They never really worship!

However, when men have genuinely accepted and encouraged each other, they should be ready to admonish one another. Having studied and discussed God's Word, they should have discovered where they really are and where they really need to be in Christ. Cooperation based on their mutually shared need and respect for each other's strengths should now replace old self-protective patterns as the team rounds third base.

Heading for Home

As every man is helped around the bases by his brothers, the momentum builds. Complementary skills will fall into place as men reap the benefits of teamwork, becoming the Body of Christ. As insight about life and its Author is shared, God's truth will be applied to life in a framework of mutual accountability and prayer. As brothers, the dream they had as they stepped up to the plate will be within their reach. They can become men of genuine integrity. They can become more like Christ!

Safe!

That's what the umpire will cry as the team crosses home plate, for this game is safe when it's played by the Rule Book. And that's exactly what men need to know! They need to know that after they've shared their lives, they will not be "benched" through betrayal of trust or a lack of commitment to one another. There will be nothing to fear because "perfect love casts out fear" (1 John 4:18). Therefore, as each player gives his best to God and each other, he will move out of isolation and into vital relationships. The team will know what it means to be brothers. They will grow in Christlikeness.

SUMMARY

The relational diamond, which we've proposed above and which will be developed in the chapters ahead, is a visual aid that has already helped many men pursue brotherhood with confidence. With the help of a qualified leader and the Holy Spirit, men should be able to go around the bases of mature Christian love without fear. Given enough time, they can have the confidence that they are becoming all that God intended them to be: brothers! (For an alternative view of the relational diamond, please refer to appendix 5.)

DISCUSSION QUESTIONS

1. How much time do you think it should take to go around the bases?
2. Why must acceptance and encouragement precede exhortation?
3. Do you feel free to step up to the plate? Why, or why not?

NOTES

Chapter 2
Heading for First

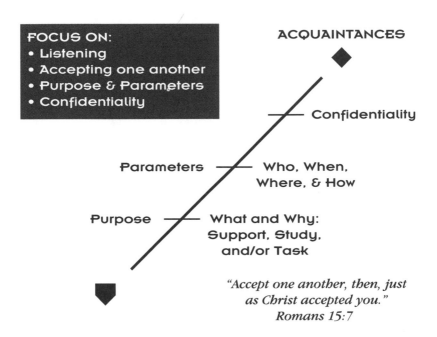

FOCUS ON:
- Listening
- Accepting one another
- Purpose & Parameters
- Confidentiality

ACQUAINTANCES

Confidentiality

Parameters — Who, When, Where, & How

Purpose — What and Why: Support, Study, and/or Task

"Accept one another, then, just as Christ accepted you."
Romans 15:7

Many years ago, I wanted to start a men's small group to study the life of Christ and to deepen our commitments to Him and to one another. There was a study guide to prepare, and we planned to meet weekly for one year in the hope of working our way around the bases and through the booklet.

We were ready to make such a commitment because we already knew each other through church-related activities: the softball games, the picnics, the coffee and doughnuts and, of course, the shared worship. Trust was there because of the time we had spent together, and we were looking forward to becoming even better friends.

A few days before we started, however, another fellow who was new to the congregation heard about our plans and invited himself to join in. Because of his warmth and enthusiasm and because of our naiveté, we overlooked the obvious. What was a natural level of communication for us would not feel natural to a stranger. As a result, since he was not at ease with the discussion, we weren't either. After a couple of months, the group seemed to stagnate, and again, because of our inexperience, we didn't know why.

❖

Since then, years of experience have taught me that everyone in the group has to be prepared for the group's *purpose*, what you are going to do and why. And the only way to do that is to invest time in listening to each other's expectations. That's what first base is all about.

As the relationships form at an acquaintance level, the basic tone of the group should be "getting to know you." The purpose is to work at accepting one another as Christ accepts us. In this atmosphere, men can explore the potential of the group and the options being offered. This takes time!

It may be that the best way to do it is around a Sunday afternoon picnic or back-yard barbeque. Other options for activities include painting a house together, hunting, fishing and the myriad of cultural and sporting events which can capture men's interest and stimulate some light conversation. Men more than women seem to need these activities to begin the trust-building process. This need is due primarily to the basic difference in the way men and women view closeness.

The Profile of a Loner
Though men will form teams to play sports, or form partnerships to make profits, and even run in gangs for self-protection, they are still loners. Why? Because of the importance of personal space to a man and how that affects his felt need for emotional closeness to another person. The term that best describes the issue in question is *intimacy*. Though some men are good at it, as a general rule, most men are not.

In his book *Uneasy Manhood*, Robert Hicks quotes Harvard researcher Carol Gilligan: "Women view closeness in positive ways, men view it as a threat. On the other hand, women view social distance as abandonment, but men view it as safety."[1] For most men, therefore, coming together in a small group to discuss life in general and their life in particular is an uncomfortable experience.

As men relinquish their personal space, even in the best of relationships they will tend to protect themselves by trying to recapture or redefine it. The challenge of the men's small group, therefore, is to learn to work with these tendencies in a positive way: in essence, to allow men to be men!

Dan Schaffer has identified five tendencies men demonstrate in their relational patterns. Admittedly, they vary greatly with each man depending upon his temperament, personality, and background. In general, however, these tendencies must be taken into account if the men are to become brothers and help each other grow in Christ.

1. *Facts.* Men often communicate by asking questions and seeking more facts. They want to get to the bottom line so that they can move on to the next goal or issue. Though this may be helpful in problem solving, it does not lend itself to intimacy. However, if men learn to ask each other good questions, with time they can deepen their relationships.

2. *Competition.* In general, men compete, women complement. Therefore, a healthy men's group will probably have more than the occasional clash of ideas and opinions. However, where very clear goals that lead to team-building can be established by a mature leader, relationships can progress. As the men see the benefits of becoming a team, they can rise above the competition and begin to channel their differences into mutual edification, appreciation, and understanding. But again, that will take time.

3. *Logic.* This is not the best term for it, but the concept it represents is in contrast to intuition. That is, men more than women process their circumstances one step at a time in a linear fashion. While most women can intuitively arrive at a conclusion about the potential of a relationship, most men can't. They need to think about it awhile.

To help them do that, men will need very clear relational goals that are identified in progressive steps. However, following those steps will take time, and any attempt to rush the process will run into the next two self-protective tendencies in male relational patterns.

23

4. *Rules.* In general, men are more preoccupied by principles or rules than they are by relationships. Though this tendency can bring order to a chaotic situation, it can also bring emotional distance. That is, men can structure meetings in such a way that everyone can avoid developing relationships if they so desire. Most women would find this unacceptable. Therefore, once order and direction have been established, rules and other structure should be kept to a minimum so the male relational process can continue.

5. *Anger.* Though women usually feel free to express their emotions in a broad range of responses, most men do not. For example, though the primary emotions felt may be pain or frustration, rather than resort to a more animated conversation or tears, most men will express these feelings in anger, even rage! A men's group is going to have to learn to deal with that if it's going to make relational progress.

Purpose and Parameters

For all of the above reasons, therefore, we came up with the relational diamond. It gives men the logical steps they need to take in a relational process that moves toward increasing intimacy. Also, it allows their goal orientation and sense of competition to express itself in positive team-building instead of divisiveness. It helps keep the rules to a minimum and emphasizes what the game is all about: relationships! In essence, when the players are well coached, it allows the men to be who they really are and to relate to one another in a comfortable way.

But even with all that, men will need time. And at first base, they will also need activities to start the trust-building that the team will need to go around the bases. In such a relaxed atmosphere, the basic purpose of the group can be discussed and agreed upon. Also, certain parameters, such as who will come and where and when the group will meet, can be determined as the level of shared interest rises.

The basic idea to remember, however, is that men will be attracted to a group if they feel comfortable with the men and agree to their purpose. Usually, that purpose will contain one or more of the following elements: *support, study,* and/or *task.*

Support is already implicit in the nature of the group's activities. The men are learning to "be there" for each other as they discuss the family, the job, the bills, and the stress-filled routines of normal life in the United States. If support is the only purpose of the group, however, some men may feel that they want something more.

In that case, the group may choose to *study* and discuss aspects of the Bible that relate to their specific situations. As their relationships deepen, they can help one another apply what they are learning to their lives.

However, if there are men who want to do something else, a *task* such as putting a new roof on the church sanctuary or organizing a fund-raiser for the local home for unwed mothers should be considered. The men may also choose to invest all their time in the the very worthy task of prayer. All the men, however, need to eventually agree on the group's purpose if it is to progress around the bases.

For example, Promise Keepers is a ministry dedicated to uniting men through vital relationships to become godly influences in their world. Promise Keepers are committed to this ministry of reconciliation to God in every area of their lives. They are men who:

1. Honor Jesus Christ through worship, prayer, and obedience to His Word in the power of the Holy Spirit.
2. Pursue vital relationships with a few other men, understanding that they need brothers to help them keep their promises.
3. Practice spiritual, moral, ethical, and sexual purity.
4. Build strong marriages and families through love, protection, and biblical values.
5. Support the mission of their church by honoring and praying for their pastors and by actively giving their time and resources.
6. Reach beyond any racial and denominational barriers to demonstrate the power of biblical unity.
7. Influence their world, being obedient to the Great Commandment (love—Mark 12:30-31) and the Great Commission (evangelism—Matthew 28:19-20).

Clear-cut purposes like these provide a fairly simple foundation upon which to build a men's group. The study part centers around what God's Word says about integrity, our marriages, kids, church, etc. The task portion could evolve into doing something for the needy and fatherless as well as crossing racial barriers. The process of studying and applying God's Word in real life and praying for each other forms much of the support we need.

Who Should Be in the Group?
Essentially, Jesus had two kinds of ministries: an open ministry to all who wanted to come and a closed ministry to a few who were ready for it. In that light, there are really only two issues that need to be addressed in this section. The first is, who should be in the group? And the second, should others be permitted to join after the group has already started (reached one or more of the bases)?

With respect to who should be in the group: When you're beginning, you have the luxury of asking whomever you want. Probably, you will choose men whom you would like to get to know better. Perhaps you have been given a random list of men who indicated they wanted to be in a men's study. Don't worry. When you have clearly determined the purpose of the group together, men will usually commit if they feel that they've been listened to and their ideas respected.

Affinity or Diversity?
Groups that initially seem to blend easier and "get around the bases" quicker will be comprised of men with similar interests: those who are in the same station (age and ages of children) in life and those who are at the same relative level of spiritual maturity. They can readily identify with each other's struggles, pressures of raising teens, marital conflicts, job pressures, etc. They seem to be able to sense what is going on in one another's lives.

However, simply because an affinity group is easier doesn't make it better. Another option is to have a group based on ethnic, cultural, or socio-economic diversity. God made each of us unique, and the potential for spiritual growth increases as we step out of the emotional comfort of our affinity groups and team up with men who are different from us. For more on how to approach cultural diversity, please refer to chapter 7, which speaks in some detail of the reconciliation process.

Open or Closed?

The second issue to address is that of permitting others to join once the group has already begun. During the acceptance phase on the way to first base, newcomers may join without much disruption if they agree with the group's purpose. After men have gone on to second or third base, however, they will not feel the same freedom to authentically share their lives with a stranger. An appropriate solution may be for the newcomers to begin another group.

When you want to get started, how do you know who will want to take part? Here's a time-tested suggestion: Ask them. You might try something like this:

> "I want to get connected with a group of men that I know on a regular basis. So here's what I'm doing. I'm calling around seven or eight guys to invite them to be a part of a men's group. We'll meet from 6:30–7:45 every Friday morning at Denny's in their back room. I've never led a group before, but I'm willing to give it a shot. I thought we'd see what the Bible says about becoming men of integrity, being better husbands and fathers—you know. We'll spend some time praying, and then we'll be on our way to work. I thought we'd try it for six weeks and then see where we wanted it to go from there. What do you think?"

The men you are inviting will either ask a few questions and say yes or make a few excuses and say no. That's no problem because you are looking for men who share your motivation to be what God wants them to be and are willing to do something about it.

Where and When Do We Meet?

Finding a place is probably the easiest decision to make. For a group that is just beginning, it is probably best to start in a restaurant or similar environment. Most restaurants have tables large enough to hold a small group of five or so. If the group is large, or if the members feel they need to have more privacy in order to share and pray, there may be a small banquet room available to meet in.

Why a restaurant? It makes double use of your time since we

all have to eat anyway. As a note of interest, the majority of Jesus' teaching took place over a meal. As the group rounds the bases, you may want a more private setting like a home or office, which will allow the men to more fully express their feelings. (The potential of meeting in a home will be developed in chapter 3.) Most men find it convenient to meet one morning a week before work. But a biweekly schedule is also feasible.

What to Do and How to Do It

As you establish your purpose, it is helpful to think of your use of the group's time together in four complementary quadrants.

The first quadrant represents a time of sharing. After the men have known each other for a while, they will want to tell each other what has been going on in their lives since the last meeting. On the way to first, the goal of the sharing time is not that the men would feel *vulnerable* (as some would suggest) but that the men would feel *comfortable* while they talk about their lives.

When men feel comfortable in an atmosphere of safety, they will open up and be authentic. The goal, therefore, is acceptance and understanding, not confrontation. That will come later and, at the right time, it will be very beneficial to the growth of the entire group.

The second quadrant represents a time in God's Word. We want to hear and discuss what God says about our lives. This quadrant is for Bible study and discussion. (Please refer to appendix 3, "The Joy of DSI: Discovery, Sharing, and Interceding")

The third quadrant represents prayer time—praying for one another and mutual concerns brought up during the sharing and Bible study. Many groups find it helpful to keep a journal of answers to prayer. This encourages praise and thankfulness.

The fourth quadrant represents our task—our mission of growing in Christlikeness and any special activities in the church or in the community which that may imply.

As the group moves around the bases, the proportions of the quadrants will shift. Your first few meetings may center on just getting to know one another. After a while, the Scriptures can be introduced. As the group matures, the quadrants may be more balanced. If you are centered on a task, the task portion may take up much of your time. Certain meetings may revolve entirely around prayer. In any case, flexibility is the key. For more discussion of the parameters, please refer to chapter 8 on trouble-shooting the small group, "The Equipment Closet."

Remember

You need to know that men will come into the group consciously or unconsciously asking themselves four questions:

1. Do I like these men?
2. Do they like me?
3. Do I agree with their goals?
4. Will I commit myself to these men?

Knowing this, you need to constantly remind yourself that what is really important at this phase are the relationships that are developing. On the way to first base, therefore, we need to focus on three issues: getting to know each other, listening, and confidentiality.

Getting to Know One Another

Our focus is on accepting each other wherever we are in life. Though activities do not guarantee acceptance, they can certainly facilitate it if the attitudes are right. Since the goal of any activity at this phase is to get to know each other better, let's move into our second objective in getting to first base.

Listening!

The key to good listening is to put our own agenda on hold. Unfortunately, just the opposite usually happens in our culture. There are three poor listening skills that are modeled around us every day. In fact, they confront us so regularly that we may not even be aware that we use them ourselves.

The first one is *shallow* listening. We're doing this when we fake interest in what the other person is saying so that our own agenda will have an opportunity to surface later. This is a control issue. This listening technique contains all the standard head nods and "unh-huhs," but the mind isn't engaged, let alone the heart. It's fake authenticity.

The second way we listen poorly is through *selective* listening. That is, we focus on our interests and what we want to hear by asking questions designed to control the discussion. We filter the information through our grid of experience, pseudo-wisdom, and world view. We don't really want to understand where the other fellow is coming from; we think we already know.

The third way we don't really listen is to be *self-protective* by avoiding any threatening messages. Any areas of discomfort can be avoided again by the artful dodge of a well-placed question. Men are masters at this. This allows them to steer the conversation far away from their personal discomfort without revealing how they really feel. Fortunately, we are not condemned to take these faulty patterns of communication into the group with us if we will begin to apply what the Scriptures say about the communication process.

To listen well, we must remember that it is an attitude, not an activity. It is a sign that indicates our dependence upon God and one another in humility.

> Do nothing out of selfish ambition or vain conceit, but in humility consider others better than yourselves. Each of you should look not only to your own interests, but also to the interests of others. (Philippians 2:3-4)

The real issue in listening is simply to esteem the other men worthy of our full attention and try our best to understand where they are coming from. Those in the communication field call this "empathetic listening."

Empathy is different from sympathy. Sympathy is feeling sorry for someone. Empathy is feeling what another person feels based on our own experiences. You cannot fake empathy. To listen empathetically takes time and effort as we seek to pick up on the emotional tone of the speaker.

You may have a good marriage, but can you empathize with a man whose wife has just left him? You may have a great job, but can you empathize with the pain of a man who has been out of work for eight months?

Without empathetic listening, we might as well be talking to a wall. For men to feel accepted they need to feel that they are really being listened to and are being taken seriously. (For more on empathetic listening, please refer to appendix 6.) Without that, no progress will be made.

Creating Confidentiality

Trust takes time to build but can be destroyed in an instant. Even an innocent remark like, "Pray for old Joe; he's really going through it" can come back to haunt the group. Don't do it!

For men to feel safe and move on to second base, they need to know that the things they share will not go beyond the group. Trust is difficult to build, but it is even harder to rebuild. Trust is a precious commodity to be protected at all costs. Once trust is gone from a group, there is little chance of moving on in the quest for Christlikeness. So agree to a *covenant of confidentiality.* Without it, other covenants can't follow.

SUMMARY

To get safely to first base, the team needs to focus on the relationships. They need to get to know each other by learning to listen empathetically. This, coupled with some interesting activities, builds the trust upon which a covenant of confidentiality can be secured. Where the relationships are progressing well, the group should be able to agree on its purpose and parameters to the point where progress can be sensed by all.

When you feel you're ready to move on to second base, however, here's a way to evaluate whether or not you've safely reached first.

1. Has communication moved from guarded to relaxed?
2. Are you beginning to know the others as persons, where they have come from and where they are?
3. Is the group communicating a desire to move on to the next step? If so, the group is ready to "slide into second."

DISCUSSION QUESTIONS

1. What do you think of the idea of "choosing" the members of the group? (See Mark 3:14-16.)
2. What are the strengths and weaknesses of an open or closed group? Which would you prefer?
3. Would you prefer an affinity group or one with more diversity? Why?
4. As we reviewed the listening skills, what did you notice about your listening patterns?
5. Reread Philippians 2:3-4 and discuss it with the others.

NOTES

1. Robert Hicks, *Uneasy Manhood* (Nashville, TN: Oliver-Nelson, 1991), page 52.

Chapter 3
Sliding Into Second

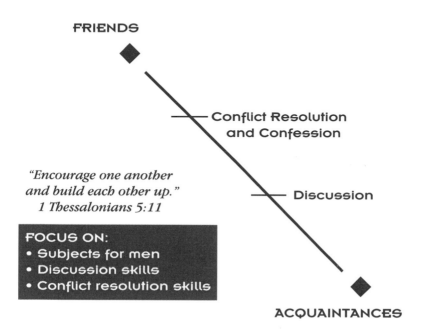

FRIENDS

———— Conflict Resolution
and Confession

*"Encourage one another
and build each other up."*
1 Thessalonians 5:11

———— Discussion

FOCUS ON:
• Subjects for men
• Discussion skills
• Conflict resolution skills

ACQUAINTANCES

A friend of mine grew up playing a variation of baseball called "bunt." The game was made up of two 2-man teams. One player would play the first base position, the other would pitch. The object was to lay down an easy bunt and then sprint toward first without getting thrown out. It sounds like fun, doesn't it? After a while, however, I think I'd want a little more. How about you?

Many small groups are like that game. Week after week, men seem content to meet with some acquaintances and do a little Bible study. And that's fine. But, life being the way it is, we need more if we're to continue to grow in Christlikeness. So let's slide into second and develop some genuine friendships.

Sliding implies friction and getting dirty! But we can't get safely to second without it. At first base, we were interested in getting to know one another. As we shared our identities and backgrounds, we worked on accepting one another in Christ; and, as best we could, we tried to listen! Because the group was new, our conversations, by design, were rather light, polite, and fairly spiritual. Everyone put on a clean uniform, so to speak, to show up for the game.

However, until those uniforms get dirty, even torn, we will not make it to second base. We need to move from being polite to being honest! Another way of saying that is, we need to "get real." This does not necessarily mean a negative experience any more than sliding is a negative experience in the game of baseball. It's just part of the game and should be accepted as such. As we move toward second, therefore, we should expect some adjustments as we rub up against each other's expectations for the group. To ensure that this friction is properly handled, we'll need skills in two areas: discussion and conflict resolution.

Discussion
The key to good discussion is to introduce relevant material, subjects that men feel they need to discuss. Also, we need to lead it in such a way that the men feel free to express what's really on their minds. Our research indicates that men are interested in discussing the following issues:

1. What is true manliness?
2. What is success? The real "bottom line" of life? Excellence?
3. How do we deal with guilt feelings?
4. What is male sexuality? Is purity possible for the modern man?
5. How can we nurture family life?
6. What is Christian leadership? How is it developed?
7. What are the basic disciplines of the Christian man?
8. What ministry skills need to be developed? How?
9. What is biblical business conduct?
10. What is integrity? How is it developed?

This is just a partial list of what is on the minds of men today. If the men are not yet comfortable with the Bible, we can recommend many books, such as *The Man in the Mirror* by Pat

Morely, which offer Christian insight into some of the above issues and are designed to be used in men's small groups.

If, however, the men are ready to discuss the Bible, one style which we would like to suggest is referred to as the DSI: Discovery, Sharing, and Interceding. (Please refer to appendix 3 for details on this method.) Here men study the Bible, discuss it, and seek to support each other in prayer as they apply what they are learning to their daily lives. Having agreed upon some relevant subjects, therefore, allow me to share with you important lessons I've learned with respect to leading a good discussion.

Shortly after I left the Air Force, I was asked by a psychiatrist to share with a small group of veterans what I had learned about life and God from my experiences in Vietnam. The doctor felt that my story would provoke their thinking if I shared a religious perspective on that sad era. Well, it sure did!

As I told them about being a pilot in Vietnam, they politely listened while I identified with their sense of loss and pain. However, what I said next had the effect of pulling the pin on a grenade. "As tough as it was," I concluded, "I grew in my knowledge of life and God."

"What's that got to do with me?!" one veteran exploded. "I didn't meet God there."

Another said, "Why did God let it happen in the first place?" And on it went, their anger at God focused on me.

Both the doctor and I were caught off guard by their reaction. Although the discussion ended with the relationships still intact, the thought that God could be there for them in the hard times was lost in their unresolved bitterness and despair.

❖

What did I learn? Much more than I bargained for! First of all, people have to be ready for a subject. If they aren't, they'll take it out on the one who brings it up. As the above story shows, this can lead to much unnecessary pain for everyone.

Secondly, I learned that it's not always what people say that matters, but how you choose to interpret it that counts. After the above discussion, the doctor and I had to deal with our own disappointment and hurt. After an hour of helping each other process our emotions, we came to the conclusion that we had honestly done the best we could. We'd been truthful but sensitive. That mutual assurance somehow let us get on with our day, even though a room full of veterans could not agree with us.

I pass these two fundamentals on to you along with the following counsel for leading a good discussion. There are four kinds of questions that are asked during discussions. Two are helpful and two are not.

1. Leading questions rarely stimulate dialogue. For example, "Of course you all agree that. . . ." The answer is usually a simple "yes" or "no," and the discussion dies there.

2. Limiting questions also inhibit discussion in that they make people guess what the person who asked the question is thinking. An example of this would be, "What are the three great truths of this passage?" Normally, people do not enjoy mind reading; and men, in particular, prefer the facts and the stimulation of questions that bring facts to light.

3. Open questions stimulate the discovery of facts about people, places, results, methods, and so on. The key words are those of the investigative reporter: who, what, when, where, why, and how. Some examples are: "Who is this all about?" "When did it take place?" "What does it mean?" "Why is it important?" These questions prepare us for the best questions, which cause us to relate the text to our daily lives.

4. Wide-open questions encourage men to voice their own opinions on how the text is relevant to life. At this phase of the group's development, that's vital. Examples would be, "What seems to be the most important thing in the passage to you, and why?" "What do you others think about that?"

With the help of wide-open questions, men will usually begin to say what they really think. Only in this way can a group move from mere acceptance to active encouragement, from being acquaintances to becoming friends.

What Is a Friend?
In Ecclesiastes 4:9-12, Solomon writes of the value of a good friend:

Two are better than one, because they have a good return for their work: If one falls down [emotionally, physically, morally, or spiritually], his friend can help him up. But pity the man who falls and has no one to help him up! . . . Though one may be overpowered [by failure, divorce, job loss, etc.], two can defend themselves. A cord of three strands is not quickly broken.

Our English word for encourage means "to fill with courage," which is what we all need to face life. The writer of the book of Hebrews says:

Let us consider how we may spur one another on toward love [our motive] and good deeds [our actions]. Let us not give up meeting together . . . but let us encourage one another. (Hebrews 10:24-25)

In essence, both men are saying that we need to have quality relationships, men who know one another well enough to "fill each other with courage." Whether it be an arm around the shoulder or a kick in the pants, friendship and encouragement go together. However, most men become friends by going through a "storm" together. This encourages honesty and develops mutual respect.

Expect Conflict!

Men will disagree about the style of the group, unmet expectations, differing goals, personality quirks, disagreements on doctrine, an unkind word, self-righteous condemnation, personal struggles at home . . . you name it. Conflict has many sources and always will be a part of life. How we manage conflict, however, determines whether we will make it to second, scramble back to the safety of first base, or drop out of the game altogether. The following story illustrates what that means.

❖

He walked into the room very upset by what he had heard on the news. A man who was convicted of multiple murders had just been executed and he wasn't sure if his conscience could accept capital punishment. He demanded to know where everyone else in the group stood! He wasn't sure he could accept a God who advocated such a thing or brothers who affirmed it.

"Why do you feel the way you do?" the leader asked.

And he went on to explain his family's painful history with the penal system. Using some rough language, he explained how flawed it was and how desperately it needed to be reformed. Obviously, this was an area that he felt strongly about because his family had been so hurt by it. The group readily accepted that as part of his uniqueness before God, but it was also his *blind spot.* That is, his emotions were so strong in this area that being objective was just not possible.

In the discussion that ensued, however, those feelings were respected. He was assured that he had a right to an opinion. But to conclude that God or his brothers were flawed if they did not agree with him was not appropriate, and his brothers humbly reminded him of that. "After all," one of them said, "if two men agree on everything, one of them is not thinking!"

❖

The group needs to remember that. Conflict is good in that it forces us to leave our comfort zones and move toward authenticity. Just as we all tested the limits of our parents' love, the small group will also be tested. Will we stand with each other or will we desert each other when conflict comes? That's the issue to be resolved on the way to second base.

You might think of it this way: On the way to first base, the group is dependent on the player-coach for group structure and content. Conflict at second base is a way of expressing independence. Conflict is saying, "Let's get real!" Moving on toward third and on to home requires interdependence—mutual respect and cooperation. Just as we need good listening skills in order to get to first base, we need skills in conflict resolution to get safely to second.

Conflict Resolution
The Chinese character for "crisis" is the symbol for "danger" superimposed on "opportunity." Conflict in a group can provide new opportunities for growth or the danger of broken relationships. Therefore, how we manage it makes all the difference. Resolving conflict is a matter of "speaking the truth in love," which should

lead to deeper understanding and growth (Ephesians 4:15). When conflict comes, our attitude must be a strong desire to learn from one another and enhance the relationship. To ensure that, we should ask ourselves the following questions before we move into a "storm" with a brother.

- ◆ Do I want to help him or hurt him?
- ◆ Is the timing right to help him grow?
- ◆ What are the pressures on his life at present?
- ◆ What is he afraid of losing?
- ◆ Am I ready to help him if he responds positively?
- ◆ Am I emotionally ready to handle his anger if he doesn't?
- ◆ What are my motives?

If I am not genuinely ready to help him, then I probably am not the man who should confront him on his attitudes or his actions. If the answers to the above questions lead me to confront in love, then I need to be sensitive to how I do it. The following is offered as a guide to where our focus should be.

1. *Focus on one problem, not many problems.* When we're upset with a brother, we need to make sure that we have a single constructive criticism in mind, not a litany of complaints. Since men need to process what they are hearing, they need something concrete to deal with. Too many inputs at any one moment lead to confusion and an emotional response. In the book of Revelation, before Jesus offered one constructive criticism to His churches, He made sure that they knew what He appreciated about them as well. So should we.

2. *Focus on the problem, not the person.* Often we are so emotionally upset that we tend to lash out at an individual's personality or character instead of helping him understand what he says or does that frustrates the group's progress. We must take the time in prayerful reflection to carefully choose our words. The goal is not to discourage the man but to help him grow. We all have blind spots. That does not excuse our behavior, but it does allow others to give us the benefit of the doubt. Shouldn't we do the same?

3. *Focus on specifics, not generalities.* We tend to generalize when we're upset. "You always . . . I never . . ." etc. Prayerful reflection demands that we don't lash out with vague generalities that

cannot be responded to in a constructive way.

4. *Focus on "I" statements, not "you" statements.* Each one of us must own our feelings and take responsibility for them. Normally, when we're upset, we accuse the other person with "you" statements such as, "You put me down!" However, if we say, "I may be too sensitive but, when that happened, I felt put down," this does not accuse the person or his character, but it does help him reflect upon his behavior in a specific, positive way.

5. *Focus on understanding, not winning.* The goal of any conflict is greater understanding. Though that seems to be impossible when we consider how competitive men are, it isn't. Where God's Spirit is at work, men can understand and eventually appreciate each other. However, the process takes time!

Remember

Conflict always involves an issue to be resolved and the people who are involved. Because of the value of people, always work toward preserving and enhancing the relationship. It's possible to win the argument and lose a friend. If you have a choice between winning the argument and winning a friend, we'd suggest that you win the friend.

All of the above help us to *suspend judgment!* While we're doing that, let's pray, seek counsel, and choose our words wisely and well. The person we are upset with represents the Body of Christ. Let's treat him accordingly. If, after prayerfully weighing our own motives and words, we find that something must be said, the Spirit of God will help us say it. "But the fruit of the Spirit is love, joy, peace, patience, kindness, goodness, faithfulness, gentleness and self-control" (Galatians 5:22-23). We must learn to count on Him.

Confession

A big part of resolving conflict is having the humility to confess to one another. That is, as we approach second base we'll need to know how to practice confession: asking forgiveness when we wrong a brother and extending forgiveness when someone wrongs us. Paul wrote in Ephesians 4:32 that we should forgive one another, just as God has forgiven us.

How has God forgiven us? Completely! Not only has He forgiven us, but He has forgotten our sin (Hebrews 10:17). How many times should we forgive our brother who sins against us? Jesus answered, "Seventy times seven." That means that the group must learn to live in a state of mutual and continual forgiveness.

But what about anger? What about those times when we've waited too long to face the issues that divide us or times when we let the anger build until it is too late and we explode and walk off in a huff?

Men do that when they have never learned to *express* their frustration in a more positive way; and if we don't control our anger constructively, it will control us. There are two ways we fail to deal with our anger—we *repress* it, or we *suppress* it.

We *repress* our anger at a subconscious level. Because of our temperament or background, we don't feel the freedom to express anger in any way. How we really feel about an issue, attitude, or action does not surface until it's too late.

The same is true for those who *suppress* their anger. What others do subconsciously, the man who suppresses his anger does consciously. Because it's related to friends, a man may come up with conscious reasons—rationalizations—for swallowing his anger. That works fine for a while.

In either case, a man's body will let him know that he has not taken responsibility for his emotions. Fatigue and other chronic symptoms, including digestive problems, should tell us that we have not expressed our emotions properly. These physical symptoms, however, are nothing compared to the damage that bitterness can cause if it is not healed by the Spirit.

To be healed we must *confess*. Jesus said:

If your brother sins against you, go and show him his fault, just between the two of you. If he listens to you, you have won your brother over. . . . For where two or three come together in my name, there am I with them.
(Matthew 18:15-20)

Jesus expected the brothers to disagree—even fight! However, He also promised that those who dared to deal with their emotions in a responsible manner would find His Spirit in their midst. God will provide the grace to get on with the game if we will only play by the rules.

The following rules of reconciliation were inspired in part

by the work of Dennis Rainey, which appears in *The Home Builders Study Guide*. First of all, we must seek the forgiveness of God and our brother when we have been wrong. We do so three ways:

1. By communicating that we understand how we hurt our brother. "I'm sorry for what I did (or said) the other day; I didn't realize how much that would hurt you . . . etc."
2. By asking him to forgive you. (Use the word "forgive"!) "Please forgive me for being so insensitive, etc."
3. By being specific. It shows you understand. "I'm sorry for implying that you could not be trusted when I said. . . ."

Second, we must grant forgiveness when we have been wronged, whether it has been asked for or not! If we don't, *we become the prisoner of the man we haven't forgiven.* Why? Because whether in his presence or absence, we are still angrily reacting to him, thinking about him, even losing sleep over him. And he may not even be aware of it!

Like humility, true forgiveness is an attitude, not an act. By God's grace, we must work at our attitude toward this person if we are to free ourselves and the group to attain our full potential in Christ. We don't have to like him; but, in Christ, we do have to love him.

Agree to Disagree

Having confessed our anger, we are now free to resolve our differences. We begin by agreeing to disagree. That is, we are saying that our relationship is still in progress. Though we cannot agree on certain issues, we are still brothers in Christ, and we haven't forgotten that.

Second, agree to reschedule the discussion of the issue until after everyone has had more time for reflection, research and prayer. Continue to put the emphasis on what you share in common, not on the specific positions that led to strife. Allow God time to work.

Third, discuss how the differences might be approached through study, arbitration, and so on. Explore options. Often there is a lack of information on the divisive issue. By agreeing to act upon it later, we continue to make progress toward one another. We have voted for the relationship instead of against it. And that's what the game is all about!

SUMMARY

We've seen that good discussion is necessary and that a certain amount of conflict is to be expected. If we are to get to second base, there will be some stormy adjustments along the way. However, we've also seen that conflict can be controlled as emotions are controlled. Men can use their differences to bring them closer together as they learn from one another in humility. The key to it all is forgiving each other "seventy times seven." Without it, the group cannot make progress. Before we move on to third, therefore, let's take an honest look at how we're doing.

1. Has communication opened up and moved into the area of sharing deeply held opinions?
2. Are our uniforms a little dirty? Have some conflicts arisen and been resolved?
3. Do we feel there is mutual respect and trust among the members of the group? If so, we're ready for some teamwork as we head for third.

DISCUSSION QUESTIONS

1. What did you learn about discussing your differences? What does it mean to handle conflict constructively?
2. In what way has forgiveness been clarified for you?
3. Why is it costly to forgive?
4. Study Matthew 18:15-20 and comment.
5. Study Galatians 6:1-5 and comment.

NOTES

Chapter 4

Rounding Third

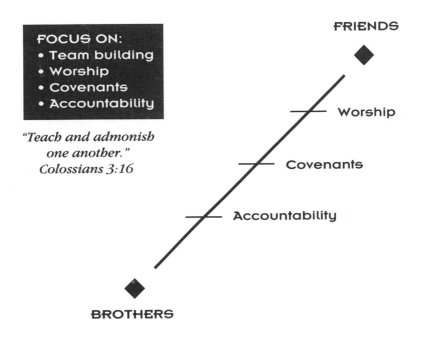

FOCUS ON:
- Team building
- Worship
- Covenants
- Accountability

*"Teach and admonish
one another."*
Colossians 3:16

FRIENDS

Worship

Covenants

Accountability

BROTHERS

The 1993 inaugural season for the Colorado Rockies was an exhilarating experience for their fans. The Rockies broke all major league attendance records as over four million fans passed through the gates. The crowd cheered when Andres Galarraga, the 1993 National League Batting champion, came to the plate, but they roared when he passed second and rounded third. Why? Because he was in scoring position.

At this point, that's where the men's group should be also. After reaching second base, the group should have achieved a new identity. After some conflict clears the air and men see the group is still together, something happens. The group changes. There are new norms of conduct. It's what athletes experience in competition. It's what soldiers feel after a battle. Men have tested the commitment of the group and it has proved genuine. They're among friends.

The theme song to the television show *Cheers* speaks of a place where everybody knows your name, where they're always glad you came, and you could share with the people there all your worries. Sounds appropriate for a great small group, doesn't it? Though we're not supposed to really admire any of the characters on the show, we may still envy the fellowship they seem to share. You see, at Cheers all of them feel free to be who they really are. And that's what makes them so interesting!

As the group approaches third base, each man should feel free to be himself as well. As they've talked and even argued, they've discovered how important those relationships really are. Together, they've learned that it's better to accept and encourage each other than it is to be "right," walk off in a huff, and abandon the game. Because of that, they can now exhort one another from the Scriptures to become the men God created them to be: brothers!

Groups should consider two more areas on the way to third base—worship and accountability. In this chapter we'll expand our concepts of worship and examine how one group of men has established a covenant of accountability with each other.

Worship in the Small Group
In the book of Acts, Luke records for us what he saw as the early church worshiped. Let's take a look:

> They devoted themselves to the apostles' *teaching* and to the *fellowship*, to the *breaking of bread* and to *prayer.* Everyone was filled with *awe*, and many wonders and miraculous signs were done by the apostles. All the believers were *together* and had everything in common. Selling their possessions and goods, they *gave* to anyone as he had need. Every day they continued to meet together in the temple courts. They broke bread in their homes and ate together with *glad* and sincere hearts, *praising* God and enjoying the *favor* of all the people. And the Lord added to their number daily those who were being saved. (Acts 2:42-47, italics added)

46

Boring and irrelevant! That's what our research reveals are the two reasons men give most for not going to church. They find the service boring and what the church does in the community irrelevant to their perceived needs. Now, having just read the preceding passage, do you have the impression that what the early church experienced was boring and irrelevant? Of course not! So what happened? They genuinely worshiped!

What is worship? Dr. Glenn Wagner offers the following helpful observations. The German word for worship means that "we minister to God as He ministers to us." The Old Testament Law wasn't given to make life boring and irrelevant. It was given to make all of life sacred! Therefore, as worship enhances our daily lives, it remains relevant. As we examine the worship of the early church, we will clearly see how genuine worship impacted their daily lives.

The above passage reveals ten facets of worship that characterized the early church. Though these were very obviously open meetings, there are certain aspects of their worship which have direct bearing upon the dynamic of a closed small group.

First of all, we see that they devoted themselves to the teaching of the apostles. They understood that to live for Christ in a secular society they had to be equipped with the Word. Paul reminds us that, "All Scripture is God-breathed and is useful for teaching . . . correcting and training in righteousness, so that the man of God may be thoroughly equipped for every good work" (2 Timothy 3:16-17).

Second, they were "devoted" to one another. Devotion is a strong word. That implies there was much more going on than just enjoying coffee and doughnuts together. For them, it was a privilege to be in each other's presence and God's.

Third, in the context of the Lord's Supper and remembering what Christ accomplished for them on the cross, they praised God and devoted themselves to prayer for one another.

Fourth, there is very little wonder, therefore, why "everyone was filled with awe." True worship ushers men into God's presence where He ministers to them. But what we see here is not the result of a ritual, but a passionate longing to be with God out of gratitude for what He'd done for them.

Fifth, God changed men as they tapped into His power. They found grace, strength, and encouragement to get on with their responsibilities as men of God.

Sixth, they were "together." They ate in each other's homes. They worshiped together. There was unity in the midst of great diversity, for worship is the great equalizer. Everything that divided them, such as race, culture, language, and socio-economic status, dissolved in the Spirit of God and the humility He inspired.

Seventh, they gave! They did not come to get, they came to give. They could do so because God had freed them of their petty preoccupations. Real goods were sold or exchanged to meet the needs of all who were there. Though none had an abundance, neither did any lack.

Eighth, there was great joy! In the midst of a world that was becoming increasingly hostile to them, there was joy. Joy is a much deeper concept than just happiness. Joy means that there was the fulfillment of having found their ultimate purpose—to glorify God. As David said in the psalm, "in thy presence is fulness of joy; at thy right hand there are pleasures for evermore" (Psalm 16:11, KJV).

Ninth, all of this spilled over into heart-felt praise for all that God was doing in their lives. And the early church found "favor" in the sight of their friends, colleagues, and acquaintances. This last fact leads us to the final point.

Tenth, true worship that transformed lives was contagious— friends and neighbors wanted in on it. Worship affected the lives of those around them as "the Lord added to their number daily those who were being saved."

Boring and irrelevant? Not hardly!

One Group's Experience

The men at Calvary Chapel in Denver, under the coaching of Jim May, have discovered that when you're in the presence of God and men's lives are changing, others want to find out more about it. Here's how Jim saw the dynamic of the book of Acts come alive in his small group.

Every Saturday morning for seven years, men sacrificed time, days off, pleasure, and sleep to get together. Often a business trip had to be cut short so that they could get back in time. Why? Because they were "devoted" to one another. Though there was no permanent leader, the meeting always had life! Men met together around the Word and relationships deepened as they

48

sought to meet each other's needs.

Each week the meeting was moved to another man's home. (Notice how the men moved into a private environment more conducive to sharing their lives.) Since that man was the host, he would take responsibility for preparing breakfast and guiding their time together in sharing and prayer. This took the pressure off one man and allowed all the men to develop their own leadership styles.

Everyone was committed to reading the Word daily, recording his thoughts about it in a journal, and sharing his observations with the group. There was no lecturing or teaching, just sharing what was on their hearts. Prayer requests were also recorded in the journal, and each man was committed to pray through them during the week. This way answers to prayer could be noted and become items for praise. (Notice how the group moved from dependence on one leader to interdependence among brothers.)

While the men ate, anything could be discussed. Here was the place for the latest scores and the latest fish story. When the meal was over, however, Scripture, sharing, and prayer became the priority. The timing and the means of this transition were up to the host.

The size of the group was limited to ten men only. Because the group was small and closed, preaching was not tolerated. Neither were secondhand thoughts. Every man got to know the others pretty well, so if the sharing was not authentic, the others usually called the man on it. "C'mon, Joe, come clean!"

In spite of this unusual level of vulnerability, however, they kept coming because they sensed the blessing of God. Their lives were changing and their marriages were being enriched. Money problems were gradually being sorted out and relationships with children were being strengthened as men rearranged their priorities.

It wasn't until much later they discovered that their group was doing most of what the early church had emphasized. But it cost them to do so. A Saturday morning was a measure of their devotion to one another. So was the way they laughed and listened to each other around the breakfast table.

Afterward, they shared in the teaching of the apostles and prayed earnestly for each other's growth in Christ. Why? Because that's what brothers are for! Boring and irrelevant? Not hardly!

Accountability

One day we'll all stand before the Lord and give an account of our lives (Romans 14:12, Hebrews 4:13). Human accountability is simply asking each other the questions on earth that God may eventually ask us in heaven. Accountability, though sometimes painful, is vital to our spiritual growth.

However, men, by our nature, despise accountability even though the testimony of Scripture is clear. Whenever men of God were in accountable relationships with likeminded peers, they thrived. When they separated themselves from other brothers or were without peer relations, they fell—morally, spiritually, or both. Think of Saul, Solomon, Demas, and so many others. But above all, think of David.

Here was God's anointed: a man "after God's own heart." He was God's choice as well as the people's choice to be king. He had the heart of a warrior and the sensitivity of a poet. Even the priests recognized that God was with David and encouraged him to do all that "God had put on his heart to do." Was David too good to be true? Absolutely not! David had spent years waging war and building the nation, but all the while, he listened to the priests and obeyed the sacred scrolls he studied.

Then one day he withdrew from it all and took a walk on the roof of his palace. There he saw a beautiful woman bathing in the court below. His emotions were inflamed and he "took her to himself." But it didn't stop there. He then contemplated and in cold blood carried out a plot to murder her husband. Watergate was nothing compared to the cover-up that followed. And it continued until the prophet Nathan confronted him. I'll let you read the rest of the story for yourself in the book of 2 Samuel.

The point I'm making, however, is that nobody is immune. Unless we are exhorting one another on a daily basis, we stand a good chance of being hardened by sin's deceitfulness (Hebrews 3:12-13). We need one another. Accountability to other men is always voluntary. We enter into accountable relationships for our benefit, and our gain will be proportionate to our honesty. So what can we do to maintain accountability?

The men of Calvary Chapel in Denver provide a model with their "Koinonia Covenant":

1. The Covenant of Affirmation: "I will love you and affirm you no matter what you have said or done. I love you as

you are for what Christ wants to make of you."

2. The Covenant of Availability: "Anything I have—time, energy, and resources—are all at your disposal. I give these to the group in a unique way."

3. The Covenant of Regularity: "I will give a regular part of my time to this group when it decides to meet. I will give that time priority on my schedule."

4. The Covenant of Prayer: "I promise to pray for you, to uphold you, and to attempt to be sensitive to the Holy Spirit concerning your needs."

5. The Covenant of Openness: "I will let you know who I am and where I am as a person in my hopes and hurts. I will need you!"

6. The Covenant of Honesty: "I will be honest in my feedback to you in what I sense and feel coming from you."

7. The Covenant of Confidentiality: "What goes on in this group stays here. I will say nothing that may be traced back to my covenant partners."

8. The Covenant of Accountability: "You have the right to expect growth from me so that you may benefit from my gifts as I do yours. You have a right to ask me questions in that regard." (For a list of questions that will help in the area of establishing mutual accountability, please refer to appendix 2.)

The above example may seem to be a bit too much for many men. However, for those who have entered into this level of accountability with their peers, the benefits have far outweighed any discomfort that such commitments may create. In a relatively short period of time, significant results can occur if the men will only commit to the process. Here's one man's story.

The Father I Never Had

I have been involved in a men's small accountability group with four other men for approximately seventeen months. This group of men has become a source of wise counsel for me, and in many ways they have become the father I never had.

I became involved with them after a Promise Keepers Conference in Boulder, Colorado. A man named Steve called me personally and asked if I would join him and a couple of other men to meet together once a week on Wednesday mornings.

My first question: "What are you going to talk about?" Steve said they'd be talking about their marriages and specifically how to be more intimate with their wives. I asked, "What do you mean, more intimate?" He explained that we would focus on Ephesians 5:25 and then allow God to direct our steps. I already knew I wanted to change my selfish attitude and be a better husband. This looked like the opportunity I'd been waiting for to do something about it.

Well, as time passed and the commitments increased, I experienced some profound personal and spiritual changes in my life. As we began to pray, study the Word, and discuss our marriages, something unique began to take place. I began to open up to these men. I discussed my pain and the lack of confidence I was feeling as a Christian man, a husband, father, and supposed spiritual leader of my home.

These men, through their counsel, "held my feet to the fire." At first, I didn't like being told what I was really like, but now I value their counsel and have given them permission to ask me some tough questions. Because of my trust of these men, my relationship with my wife is much better. I have also been able to give my father and my sons the blessing of a much deeper relationship.

I guess I can say that on my own I never would have joined an accountability group. However, after being in one for over a year, I will never be without one. Proverbs 27:17 is the verse I've chosen which best summarizes my experience with these men. It says, "As iron sharpens iron, so one man sharpens another." There were moments when the "sharpening" was very painful, but I can honestly say that the pain has been worth it.

As you can tell, I am now a zealot for guiding men into small groups because without relationship and accountability, we will never, as Christian men, reach our spiritual potential.

SUMMARY

Not everyone is ready for this kind of commitment! But it does seem to model what the early church experienced as recorded in the book of Acts. These models should not make any group feel ashamed for not having reached this level of growth; neither should they prevent anyone from starting a group at a less intense level.

We present them to show what can be done if men are ready to go further, deeper! We trust that these examples will be accepted in that light—a challenge to keep us pressing on so we won't become boring and irrelevant! In that light, here are some questions to help us evaluate where we are.

1. Are we learning from each other's strengths?
2. Are we learning to work together?
3. Have we begun to allow the group to hold us accountable?

If we can answer the above questions positively, then the group is ready to head for home.

DISCUSSION QUESTIONS
1. Why do so many men feel that their needs are not being met in the Christian community?
2. What did you notice for the first time about the early church?
3. What really spoke to you about the Koinonia Covenant?
4. How do you suppose men prepare themselves to make such a covenant?
5. How long do you think it takes to get there?
6. How do you feel about such a level of accountability? Would you like to try it? Why, or why not?
7. Reread the above text from Acts and discuss it.

NOTES

Chapter 5
Coming Home

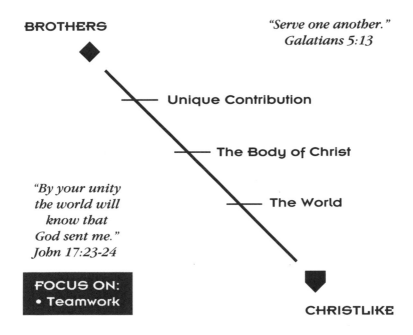

BROTHERS

"Serve one another."
Galatians 5:13

Unique Contribution

The Body of Christ

*"By your unity
the world will
know that
God sent me."*
John 17:23-24

The World

FOCUS ON:
• Teamwork

CHRISTLIKE

"Hey, guys," Steve said, grinning, "just think how far we've come. Bill, a year and a half ago your wife had just left you; and you, Nick, were out of work; and Rob—you were ready to call it quits in your marriage. We've come full circle. We've hung together, been there for each other, and we've helped each other get through to the other side. This has been great!"

Steve continued, "We all know that we couldn't have made it alone. You know, I've been thinking about the men that have gone through the same things we've gone through but don't have a group of guys to help them. Man, I'm thankful for you guys." And so was everyone else as they reflected on just how far they had come together. They were brothers!

❖

Being there for one another is important. However, as important as it is to help each other through the hard times, there is still more to this game. If you'll permit me to carry our baseball analogy just a little bit further, there's the "World Series"! Let me show you what I mean as we round third and head for home.

Jesus Had a Mission

When Jesus formed His small group it was with a twofold purpose. Jesus called to Himself those whom He wanted, "that they might be with him and that he might send them out to preach" (Mark 3:13-14). He never lost sight of His purpose.

Before they could effectively and consistently impact their world, however, the disciples needed to learn from Jesus how to work with their brothers as a team. Jesus reminded the disciples the night before His crucifixion that it was through their love for one another that the world would know they really belonged to Him (John 13:34-35). And it would be through their unity that the world would know that Jesus was sent from God (John 17:23-24). We can't bypass the brothers to reach the world, for it's as a mature band of brothers that we can reach the world! The Great Commandment, "love one another," is the key to the Great Commission.

Jesus never intended that His small group remain in Jerusalem. He entrusted a mission to them. In His last command before His ascension He gave His marching orders: "Go into all the world and preach the good news to all creation. . . . Make disciples of all nations" (Mark 16:15, Matthew 28:18-20). The book of Acts is the record of that small group of men as they were progressively transformed from *disciples* to *brothers* to *laborers* in the Kingdom of God.

How do we impact the world around us? How do we head towards home? What does it mean to move toward Christlikeness, especially as a group of stubble-faced men? To become like Christ is to allow Him to change us progressively from the inside out, to adopt His values as our values, His priorities as our priorities. In Matthew 9:36-38, we get a glimpse of Jesus' heart for the world around us.

When he saw the crowds, he had compassion on them, because they were harassed and helpless, like sheep without a shepherd. Then he said to his disciples, "The harvest is plentiful but the workers are few. Ask the Lord of the harvest, therefore, to send out workers into his harvest field."

Jesus didn't view men as losers. He saw them as lost. He felt compassion for them, and He had a solution: raise up laborers through prayer. Moving toward home means that we learn to see men as Jesus saw them, feel as Jesus felt, and do what Jesus did. How?

God has given us a means for being a worker in the harvest and a set of tools to accomplish the work. The means is His Church. The tools are our talents, strengths, abilities, gifts, and interests. In short, our tools are our uniqueness, and that is what He wants to harness for His Kingdom.

The Church—The Body of Christ

When the Apostle Paul groped for an illustration of what God's Church is like, under the inspiration of the Holy Spirit he wrote the following:

> The body is a unit, though it is made up of many parts; and though all its parts are many, they form one body. . . . The eye cannot say to the hand, "I don't need you!" And the head cannot say to the feet, "I don't need you!" On the contrary, those parts of the body that seem to be weaker are indispensable. . . . There should be no division in the body . . . its parts should have equal concern for each other. If one part suffers, every part suffers with it; if one part is honored, every part rejoices with it. Now you are the body of Christ, and each one of you is a part of it. (1 Corinthians 12:12-27)

"I don't need you!" is the cry of the loner, not the cry of the human heart. Paul knew that each person needed to belong. What the above text teaches us is that we do belong to something much bigger than ourselves, but we must have the humility to accept it. We must remember that our ultimate fulfillment depends upon others. Unless we are an integrated part of the body of believers, we will not grow in Christ. If we are connected, however, we can use our gifts and talents for the good of the team.

Interdependence

Paul chose the model of the human body because it is a marvelous example of interdependence. Each part is dependent upon the others, yet each part retains its own uniqueness to make an independent contribution to the other parts. When it is in good health, the body is so well coordinated that life support is automatic.

The Body of Christ—His Church—is designed to function in the same manner. However, the reason Paul wrote this epistle was to rebuke the church in Corinth for its divisive spirit. Every man was so caught up in glorifying his own gift or preaching his own doctrinal emphasis that he forgot he needed the others. He forgot love. He forgot to be a brother!

Honor the Body

One of the core values of the Body of Christ should be honoring the pastors and priests of our local congregations. These leaders struggle with the same things we do. They need our support, prayers, encouragement, and cooperation. We want to be catalysts to the men's ministry of the local church. For a group of men to impact the society around them, they will be most effective working through the context of their local church in cooperation with their pastors.

During the 1993 Promise Keepers Conference, Coach McCartney invited the pastors to come forward so we could pray for them. Like us, over one thousand of God's servants had come to PK '93 to learn to be men of integrity. Many wept openly because of the love and appreciation displayed that night. The pain of overwork and under-affirmation was evident. How many others, just like them, need our support?

We suggest that you regularly write notes of affirmation to the pastor of your church expressing your appreciation of him and his ministry. Many men have unrealistic expectations of their shepherds. Our pastors need our help! Gaps in the ministry of the church should be seen as an opportunity to serve, not cause for criticism. A man's man is a loyal man and a supportive man. His only interest is that God would be praised for the teamwork He creates. Peter reminds us what our gifts are for:

> Each one should use whatever gift he has received to serve others, faithfully administering God's grace in its

various forms. If anyone speaks, he should do it as one speaking the very words of God. If anyone serves, he should do it with the strength God provides, so that in all things God may be praised through Jesus Christ. To him be the glory and the power for ever and ever. Amen! (1 Peter 4:10-11)

It sounds wonderful, doesn't it? Then why do we see it so rarely? Perhaps a tattooed biker who came to the conference in Colorado can give us the answer. He told us that his attitude before he met Christ was summed up by the old rebel yell, "I'd rather rule in hell than serve in heaven!" As shocking as that attitude seems to be, many of us unconsciously cling to a similar dogma, even though we're Christians.

We're loners, and we like it that way. Apparently, it's more important for us to rule in our own small world than it is to serve a Kingdom that is so much bigger. This is what Jesus meant when He said, "count the cost" and "take up your cross and follow me" (Luke 14). There are only servants in His Kingdom. Are we willing to become one? (This will be discussed further when we come to the chapter on leadership.)

If our service is multiplied by the thousands, the world will begin to feel the full impact of the Kingdom of God. Can this be? Has Jesus really entrusted to the small group not only His presence and power, but also His mission? Can any meeting of mere men really be that significant?

Perhaps the best way to illustrate this point is to tell the old story that comes down through the ages by way of church folklore. For throughout the history of the church, the implications of this incredible discovery have been the object of much debate. Lyman Coleman tells this story to illustrate just how important a committed group of men can be:

Soon after Jesus ascended to the Father, He encountered the archangel Gabriel. He wanted to know what Jesus had been doing all this time during His tenure on Earth. Jesus elaborated on the now familiar story of His life and times with particular emphasis on Good Friday and Easter Sunday—that is, the Cross and the Resurrection.

"Now that I am ascended to the right hand of the

Father," Jesus told Gabriel, "I can intercede in prayer for my beloved disciples. In short order, I will send the Holy Spirit as Comforter, Advocate and Power Source so that the message of God's Kingdom will spread throughout Jerusalem, Judea and Samaria, and the ends of the earth."

Gabriel listened intently but did not hear what he expected, so he asked Jesus, "And what, pray tell, is your plan for getting the word out?"

Jesus is imagined to have said, "I left the message with a small band of men, a motley crew of twelve. I am trusting them to spread the good news everywhere."

Taken aback by the plan's simplicity, Gabriel confronted our Lord, "And what if they fail?" To which Jesus reportedly said, "I have no other plan."

THE CHALLENGE

We cannot grow by ourselves. We must have the humility to get involved with our brothers and stay involved. As our commitment to serve God and the body of believers solidifies, the Spirit will gradually reveal to us what our contribution is to be. Then, in our own way, we can participate in what God is doing in the world today as part of a committed team of men.

When we have reached this point, we should be able to answer the following questions:

1. Are we beginning to face the challenges of life as a team?
2. Is mutual accountability becoming foundational to our lives?
3. Are we helping our churches? If so, how?
4. Are we finding the resources to reach out to our peers at work and in our communities? If so, how?

If the answers to the above questions are "yes!" then we are ready to multiply our effectiveness. We do this by encouraging yet other groups of men to "step up to the plate." This can be accomplished as members of our own team prepare to lead other groups of men around the bases. Before they do this, however, let's weigh their qualifications as leaders by discussing the next chapter, "The Servant-Leader."

DISCUSSION QUESTIONS

1. How do you think the concepts of dependence, independence, and interdependence relate to the small group?
2. How do the individual's personal abilities relate to the dynamic of the men's small group as it begins to perform as a team?
3. What did you notice about your possible contribution to the group?
4. What have others in your group noticed about your possible contribution?
5. Do you now feel ready to lead a group of men around the bases? Why, or why not?

NOTES

Chapter 6
The Coach: A Servant-Leader

After all is said and done, there is only one thing that characterizes a leader. It's more important than making things happen, setting priorities, and even hard work. It's more important than intelligence, self-confidence, energy, and knowledge. It's more important than social skills and initiative. It's more important than personality and position. No matter what we have been taught to think, the only true mark of a leader is that he has followers! Reverend E.V. Hill, pastor of Mount Zion Missionary Baptist Church, aptly stated, "He who thinks he is a leader and has no followers is merely taking a walk."

No matter how competent a man may feel in his chosen occupation, most men feel inadequate in the area of spiritual leadership in the home and among other men. If that's your case, don't get discouraged, because you are in good company. Moses gave several excuses to God why he couldn't be a leader either! So did all the disciples—before Pentecost. But, as intimidating as the word sounds, "leadership" is not that difficult. Howard Hendricks defined a leader as "someone who knows where he is going and is able to persuade others to go along with him." In that light, here are some suggestions for effective leadership of the group.

Where Are You Going?
Where do you want to go? You can't really ask a group of men to join with you if you cannot answer with clarity, "Why are we getting together?" and "What are we going to do?" A leader prepares to lead. To do so he must ask himself the following questions:

1. Who are the men God has entrusted to me?
   (See John 17:6.)
2. What are their needs?
3. How will this group meet those needs?
4. How will I know that I have ministered to those needs?
   What will they be saying, feeling, or doing after I've tried

63

to serve them in this way?

5. Where do I want the group to go?

6. What is our game plan?

Some men have a clear idea of where they would like to go but can't persuade anyone to follow them. That takes us to the second qualification of a leader, his reputation. One of the more famous quotes generally attributed to President Eisenhower is, "A leader has followers and is trustworthy."

How to Persuade People to Follow You

In their book *The Leadership Challenge,* James Kouzes and Barry Posner interviewed nearly 1500 managers from around the country and asked the following question: "What values do you look for and admire in your superiors?" The response of these professionals was disarmingly simple. What these men valued more than anything else was *honesty.* After that they wanted a man who had a sense of where the team needed to go and an idea about how to get there. This they called competence.[1]

They also reported that the same findings were true for thousands of employees interviewed at AT&T. When they were asked what they wanted most in their leaders, they replied, *honesty.* After that, they wanted a leader who had a vision for the future and could demonstrate that he knew something about how to get there. That's not asking too much, is it?

Where there's some integrity, a little vision, and knowhow, people begin to feel secure and significant. They feel that they are part of a team and that what they are doing is worthy, so they follow. Jesus summed it all up when He told His disciples:

> You know that the rulers of the Gentiles lord it over them, and their high officials exercise authority over them. Not so with you. Instead, whoever wants to become great among you must be your servant, and whoever wants to be first must be your slave—just as the Son of Man did not come to be served, but to serve, and to give his life as a ransom for many. (Matthew 20:25-28)

From Christ's perspective, a true leader is a servant, committed to the success of each individual in the group. Jesus did not criticize His disciples' desire to lead; He just showed them how to do it by washing their feet (John 13:1-7). Then He said:

> Now that I, your Lord and Teacher, have washed your feet, you also should wash one another's feet. I have set you an example that you should do as I have done for you. (John 13:14-15)

The essence of spiritual leadership, therefore, is following Jesus and serving people. People rebel against controlling leaders, but it is impossible to rebel against a servant. According to the New Testament, our motivation for service should be that of a shepherd (1 Peter 5:2-3). He watches over the flock because He really cares. Though Jesus was a carpenter by trade, He became the Good Shepherd as He cared for His flock all the way to the cross!

While serving people pertains to a task or their physical needs, shepherding has to do with how much you care for them—their emotional needs. As we've often heard, "people don't care how much you know until they know how much you care." Therefore, the spiritual leader cares. And because he cares, he's willing to serve, even if it hurts.

What a Leader Does
What we've tried to provide for you in this book is a little bit of vision and knowhow. However, it will be up to you to provide the honesty, sincerity—the heart!—of a ministry of reconciliation to men. For without it, there will be no life. You'll just be adding one more activity to an already overcrowded schedule. So, what's the key to giving life to a ministry?

Jesus said, "I am the way and the truth and the life" (John 14:6). Any genuine life in a ministry, therefore, will come from Him through the heart of the leader. A wise monk once said that the ministry is this: "It is simply giving Jesus to the people that Jesus has given to you." We bring Him into our small group as leaders when we embody the hope and life that Christ came to give all men.

To be a spiritual leader, therefore, is to minister through His resources, not our own. We cannot give away what we do not possess. If our own spiritual resources are depleted, we will have little to share with our brothers. In Luke 6:45, Jesus says, "The good man brings good things out of the good stored up in his heart. . . . For out of the overflow of his heart his mouth speaks."

Our words will be an overflow of our heart. The heart is the reservoir for spiritual resources. So what can we store up in our hearts? The answer is His Word, His Spirit, and people.

The Word of God. "I have hidden your word in my heart" (Psalm 119:11). His Word equips us for every good work (2 Timothy 3:16-17). The Scriptures give us and those in our group genuine hope. Followers need the assurance that the leader is working on his own integrity issues by listening to the voice of God in His Word. They will listen to a person who is listening to God because his life and goals will reflect God. Before a leader can speak for God to others, he must allow God to speak to him.

Jesus Christ, Himself. ". . . so that Christ may dwell in your hearts through faith" (Ephesians 3:17). This is a picture of the Spirit-filled life. Paul wrote, ". . . our competence comes from God," who made us competent by the Spirit (2 Corinthians 3:5-6). To be filled with the Spirit is to have a moment-by-moment conscious dependence on Christ. Spiritual leadership cannot be accomplished through the resources of the flesh.

People. "Make room for us in your hearts" (2 Corinthians 7:2). Do we really care for people? As we fill our hearts with concern for people, we find ourselves praying for them. The weakest link in the life of any spiritual leader is probably prayer. There are so many good things to do that we fail to do the best thing: pray! Leaders, by their natures, are activists. Therefore, they rarely bring their needs and those of others to God in prayer. What happens when we do pray? There is power. Lives change, including the life of the leader! The following acronym—ACTS—may be a helpful guideline in prayer.

ADORATION: Praising God for who He is. Reflect upon Psalms 145-150. It is often beneficial to reflect to God in worship what you learned about Him in His Word.

CONFESSION: Telling God about us—our sin, our feelings, our fears. "Lord, here's where I'm coming from this morning. . . ."

THANKSGIVING: "Give thanks in all circumstances, for this is God's will for you in Christ Jesus" (1 Thessalonians 5:18). What are you thankful for? Your wife? Your children? Your pastor? Each man in your group? Tell the Lord about it.

SUPPLICATION: This means praying for ourselves and interceding for others. God always answers our prayers—sometimes with "yes," sometimes with "no," sometimes with "wait"—and sometimes He fulfills our desire though not our specific request. However, every answer comes from the same loving hand.

Barnabas

Can you remember a man named Mordecai Hamm? I must admit that I didn't when I first heard the name. Mordecai Hamm was the man who led Billy Graham to Christ. How about the biblical character, "Joseph, a Levite from Cypress"? Again, I needed to be reminded that Joseph is better known as Barnabas. Barnabas means "Son of Encouragement," and this Christian name more accurately represents the nature of his gifts and character.

Very little is mentioned of Barnabas in Scripture. First, when the early church needed money, he "sold a field he owned and brought the money and put it at the apostles' feet" (Acts 4:37). Then, when the great Pharisee Saul of Tarsus came to Christ, the apostles avoided him like the plague, "but Barnabas took him" (Acts 9:27).

He persevered with Saul, patiently being the link between him and his destiny in Christ. He took Saul with him wherever he went, making the appropriate introductions and putting him forward until his place as one of the leaders of the church was finally recognized. Eventually, Barnabas himself was far overshadowed by Saul of Tarsus.

The New Testament records one other man whom Barnabas influenced during his lifetime—a washout of another's ministry, his cousin, John Mark (Acts 15:36-40). What kind of impact can a man like Barnabas have? What kind of impact can you or I have? You may not have very visible gifts, but if God has given you His Word, His Spirit, and a heart for people, you will have a lasting impact. God uses men of integrity and faith more than men of position and title or the other attributes so valued today.

Some of you may feel like a Saul, a future leader waiting to emerge. Then, like Saul, you need to find a Barnabas, or he needs to find you. Still others are convinced that they are more modestly gifted. That was Barnabas—an average guy with average gifts. However, he had a major advantage. He knew that God wanted to use men like him to influence other men. Though we're certain he saw potential in Saul and John Mark, who would have guessed how far Barnabas' influence would eventually reach?

Saul of Tarsus is better known as the great evangelist and apostle Paul. He wrote half of the New Testament. As for John Mark, he became a traveling companion of Peter and under the inspiration of the Holy Spirit, penned the Gospel according to Mark. You may not be a Paul or even a John Mark, but you can be a Barnabas, a brother!

SUMMARY

In the world, people are looking to follow a man who is both honest and who knows where he is going and how to get there. However, to be a coach, we must take those admirable qualities and go one step further. In the Kingdom of God, the leader is both a servant and a shepherd. To maintain his heart, he must develop certain spiritual disciplines that refine his motives: prayer, the study of God's Word, and keeping in step with the Spirit. Lastly, he must prepare to meet the needs of those who are following him. We are not all Pauls, but we can be like Barnabas and have a spiritual impact beyond measure.

DISCUSSION QUESTIONS

1. What have you noticed about spiritual leadership?
2. What disciplines would you add to those necessary for such leadership?
3. What struck you about the relationships between Paul, John Mark, and Barnabas?

LEADERSHIP SURVEY

As you begin to consider becoming a leader or choosing a leader for a small group, please prayerfully consider some of the following concerns. Have you (or the leader you are considering) been around the bases with a small group already? Have you reached the level of accountability and teamwork with those men? If so, you may want to work through the following questions with one of your brothers or your pastor to help you clarify your motives, skills, and Christian experience as a possible small group leader.

First of all, please ask yourself these two very important questions:

1. Is there anything in my past that, if it came to light, would damage the men I am trying to help?
2. Am I currently involved in some addictive behavior (sexual, chemical, work-related, etc.)?

If these questions have revealed some areas of concern, you may want to get involved in a special support group designed to help people address these issues. I think we would all agree that it would be best to wait on leading a group until these concerns have been resolved. If, however, the answers to the above questions are no, then *prayerfully* answer the following questions with the help of a brother.

Motivation

1. Why do you want to lead other men?
2. Is your behavior consistent with your Christian beliefs? What do other people think?
3. Can you look at a man and see his potential in Christ?
4. Do you tend to take yourself too seriously? What do others think?
5. Do you tend to become defensive when people disagree with you? What have others noticed?

Practical Application of Scripture

1. When reading a passage of Scripture, can you answer the questions, "What does it say?" and "What should I do?"
2. Can you use a Bible dictionary and a concordance when finding a biblical answer on a specific subject?

3. Have you ever helped, or been helped, to apply a biblical approach to a problem, even when it was difficult?

If you could answer most of the above questions "yes" most of the time, you are ready to lead a small group. However, if you answered three or more "no," you would probably be wise to "play a season" under the leadership of a veteran player-coach. In either case, what you will find in our concluding chapters will be very helpful to you as you seek to play the game more effectively.

NOTES

1. James Kouzes amd Barry Posner, *The Leadership Challenge* (San Francisco, CA: Jossy-Bass, Inc., 1987), page 16.

Chapter 7

Breaking Into the Game: The Reconciliation Process

The year was 1936. The place was Berlin. A petty dictator, who later plunged the world into war, turned his back and refused to look upon the presentation of the Olympic medals for the 100 meter sprint. Why? Because he was convinced that the men who were about to receive them were not qualified even though they had won the event! Why? They were black.

We've all seen the newsreels: Adolph Hitler turned his back to Jesse Owens, one of the greatest athletes in history, and America was shocked. But what the newsrecl doesn't show is that Hitler kept his back turned to the athletes as the silver medal was presented to another black sprinter named Mack Robinson. Mack went on to become a great inspiration to his younger brother, Jackie. And what Jackie Robinson did shocked America.

The year was 1945. The place was the office of Branch Rickey, the general manager of the Brooklyn Dodgers. After a couple of successful seasons in the "Negro League," Jackie Robinson was called into that office to "discuss something" with "Mr. Baseball." What that "something" was, however, stunned the sports world.

When Jackie walked into the office, Mr. Rickey rose to his feet, walked over to shake his hand, and then began to call Jackie the most abusive racial slurs that came to his mind. Everyone in the office was jolted, including Jackie. What they didn't know, however, was that for years Branch Rickey had been looking for the "right man" to begin the integration process of the major leagues. The reason for his abusive language was to see if Jackie would be able to take what Rickey knew the players and the public would deal out to the first black man to enter their "white only" domain.

Rickey's scouts had been right. Jackie was not only a superb athlete, but his education at UCLA and his experience as an Army officer in the Second World War had prepared him for the struggle against blind prejudice. Jackie knew he had nothing to prove to himself, and perhaps that's what freed him to prove his equality to others. Encouraged by the faith of his mother, who had persevered alone with four children, he signed the historic contract.

After a record-setting season in the minors, Mr. Rickey called Jackie up to the majors for his debut at Ebbits Field, April 15, 1947. However, the pressure was so intense that he went into a batting slump. For several games, the fans and opposing players yelled the classic insults as the opposing pitchers singled him out to be "dusted off" at the plate. Also, Jackie and his wife, Rachel, received hostile letters and phone calls, which even contained threats to kidnap their son if Jackie didn't quit.

But he didn't.

The rest is history. That year he led the Dodgers in home runs and stolen bases. In 1949 he was the National League Batting Champion and the league's Most Valuable Player. By the following year there were black players on every team in major league baseball. Jackie had won!

But no man should have had to go through the ordeal he did in order to express his God-given talents. Such racism is sin, a vile evil that pollutes a nation and its people. And yet it happened, not in a faraway land caught in the vanities of a demented dictatorship, but in a country that was supposed to be governed by a Constitution that guaranteed basic human dignity. It happened in America.

And it's still happening. Jackie Robinson's courageous entry into baseball took place almost fifty years ago. Since then, there have been other heroes on other fronts, and in the face of much social unrest, many laws have been promulgated to bring about change: freedom and equality for all men no matter what their color or creed! However, as I talked with Roger the other day, I came to the conclusion that we still have a long, long way to go.

Roger's Story

"Bring something back! That's what I wanted to do," said Roger, an engineer in a large aerospace company. "I wanted to do it for my dad, for myself, and for my people. I wanted to bring something back for us all! I wanted to be so successful that I could help out, treat people right—like my father taught me to.

"But, then I looked around at how I was being treated." He went on, and though there was sadness in his voice, there was no self-pity. "Like most black people, I had a history of being treated as something other than a normal human being. I can remember going to my first job. It was six in the morning, and I was alone in downtown Detroit waiting for the bus. It was still dark out and the bus was late.

"Suddenly, a gang of whites who were standing across the street started shouting the most abusive language at me—deliberately provocative. I was twenty-four, a college graduate who'd recently been hired by a large firm, and they were treating me as though I were...." His voice trailed off. The pain clear in his eyes, he said, "If I'd been white, it might not have even happened. But, if it had, I probably would not have been so afraid."

"Why?" I said.

"Just a generation ago," he continued, "if a gang like that decided to act out their threats with a beating or even a lynching, they probably could have gotten away with it! And that's what made me scared. Our history." Roger paused, searching for the words. "We, as a people, have a history, a history that has been told to us ever since we were old enough to listen. A history that says, 'You'd better watch out, you can't escape.'

"You see, we were slaves, but now we're guests—uninvited and unwanted guests in the white man's world. We can't escape their management style, the way they handle information, or the way they evaluate people. My father, for example, drove a forklift for thirty years because people refused to recognize that he was an educated man. After he'd saved up a down-payment for a home, he was refused a loan because he was the wrong color.

"Though that kind of thing is against the law today, it still happens in subtle ways. That's the 'glass ceiling' everyone talks about. You can see the way out of the inner city or even the way to the top of the corporation, but you just can't get there. It appears to be reserved for someone else. Someone white.

"Our history says that whatever our host wants to do to us, he can do, and until recently, there was very little we could do about it. That's pain, man, real pain—ingrained in the system and inescapable." He paused again, searching for the words that could somehow make me understand. "When people see the ghetto explode in flames, they're shocked and demand, 'How can this happen?' My response to that is, in light of all that has happened, why doesn't the inner city explode more often?!"

"Is there any hope?" I asked.

Roger surprised me when he said, "I don't believe integration or affirmative action is going to get us there. It has to go deeper than that—much deeper. The way I see it, the white man has a lot of history to repent of and make amends for. But we have a lot of history to forgive, particularly if we are going to escape the hopelessness of the 'victim mentality.' I don't know which will be harder, but God help America if we don't!" And with that, Roger stared right through me.

After a few awkward moments, I humbly suggested that we pray for reconciliation. And we did. In the process, I honestly believe that a few halting first steps were taken on a long, long journey toward a brotherhood made possible in Christ.

There's where true reconciliation starts—at the Cross! There is no brotherhood of man without the universal Fatherhood of God. And that's what Roger and I discovered in my office that day. In spite of the history that separated us, there was a greater power that united us: Christ's love for all men.

I knew that if I would only let it, His love could lead me to repentance. And Roger knew that if he would only let it, Christ's love could lead him to forgiveness. As we shared our very divergent lives that day, our common heritage in Christ became the bridge to reconciliation. Only the Cross was powerful enough to break down the walls of pride.

The Four Faces of Pride

At the top of the list of the attitudes and actions that are most detestable to God is what the Scriptures call "haughty eyes" (Proverbs 6:16-17). In another passage, the psalmist reminds us that, "You [the Lord] save the humble, but bring low those whose eyes are haughty" (Psalm 18:27). What does that mean?

"Haughty eyes," which is translated elsewhere as the "prideful look," means that our concept of who we are as a person or as a people is not in line with reality—who God says we are! Paul warned us against pride when he said, "Do not think of yourself more highly than you ought, but rather think of yourself with sober judgment" (Romans 12:3).

As a Pharisee, Paul knew exactly what that meant. Self-deceiving pride keeps us from listening to and learning from our brothers. And that's why God "hates" it so. Pride manifests itself in four distinct ways: face, place, grace, and race.

Face has to do with our outward appearance, the physical attributes of a man. How does he look? In North America, with our accent on advertising and "image," there is little wonder why people now pay more attention to the package than to its contents. The "beautiful people" will always tend to look down on others. We must ask ourselves if we are one of them?

Place speaks of a man's station in life: his position, power, perks, and parking place. In reference to this, the psalmist warns that the successful will be tempted to pride. "His ways are always prosperous; but he is haughty and your laws are far from him" (Psalm 10:5). The prosperous man will tend to look down upon those who are less so and forget who he really is before God. Are we like him?

Grace. How could God's grace or favor lead to pride? The same way it blinded the eyes of Israel to their own Messiah. They were the chosen, and they knew it! They knew God, and they didn't need a humble carpenter to tell them about God's Kingdom. This was particularly true for the Pharisees, the branch of the Jews that Paul represented. Until God blinded him, Paul looked down upon a new branch of Judaism called the Christians because he thought he knew God better than they did. Do we do the same?

Lastly, the most obvious manifestation of pride is *race*. Race is more than just reacting to the color of a man's skin. It's a "we-they" tribalism. And when that's pushed to the limit, it's called chauvinism. At that point, "we" are righteous and "they" are not. "We" are superior and "they" are inferior. We think "we're" better. And because of that, "we" can treat "them" differently in the streets, in the markets and, as Roger reminded us, even in the courts of law.

Racism is not new. Certainly Jesse Owens felt its sting that day in Berlin. But in the U.S., which was founded on the concepts of freedom and equality, racism stands out as a shocking revelation of the human heart. Are we looking down on a man with our "haughty eyes" because of his color or his accent? Do we have a right to do so in a land that speaks so much of rights? Not if we're one of Christ's ambassadors.

And he died for all, that those who live should no longer live for themselves, but for him who died for them and was raised again. . . . Therefore, if anyone is in Christ, he is a new creation; the old has gone, the new has come! All this is

75

from God, who reconciled us to himself through Christ and gave us the ministry of reconciliation. . . . And he has committed to us the message of reconciliation. We are therefore Christ's ambassadors, as though God were making his appeal through us. We implore you on Christ's behalf: Be reconciled to God. (2 Corinthians 5:15-20)

The Principle of Intentionality

An ambassador represents his king. In the diplomatic world, an ambassador is asked to convey the king's message as accurately as possible wherever he may be sent. To do this, he must first learn the king's message. Then, he must be ready to leave his tribe and his people to cross borders and interact with other cultures and traditions. Often he must go through the painful and humiliating process of learning to speak another language. However, it's only by making such a conscious effort that an ambassador succeeds. He must intend in his heart to surmount all obstacles to his mission: to represent his king.

The same holds true for us. Only with similar intentions, focus, and purpose can a man abandon his "haughty looks" to see more clearly how to cross the barriers to brotherhood in the U.S. today. Obviously, there are risks. But, there are also great rewards. Consider how Dan Schaffer saw it as he began to work with Ray Vialpando, an Hispanic American:

"I met Ray on his first day in the office. The first thing that I noticed about Ray was that he seemed to have unlimited energy. As we introduced ourselves, I asked him if that twinkle in his eye wasn't a sign of how he related to life and his colleagues. He admitted that it might be, and we began to get to know each other. We made an effort to work together on projects, such as meeting other pastors in the minority community and teaching workshops. As time passed, I began to sense that there were a lot of things that we shared in common.

"We were both committed to allowing God to make us into the men we should be. We shared a deep commitment to our families and wanted to see our children know God intimately throughout their lives. Finally, we also shared an infectious sense of humor. We joked and laughed, and through the time together we were able to develop trust that enabled us to begin to share our lives more intimately.

"We found that we were from very different theological backgrounds; one was a Pentecostal, and the other was from a more conservative evangelical tradition. We also found vast differences in our educational and occupational training. However, we also noticed that each one of these discoveries brought richness and depth to our relationship. As we learned to trust each other more, I noticed that we began to value these differences instead of fear them. We learned from one another!

"I was able to experience with Ray what it was to go from being acquaintances to being friends to, finally, becoming brothers. I know now that in the past I have missed out on the richness God had for me in this area. Because of minor prejudices and fears—'haughty looks' and their justifications—I didn't take the time I should have to discover my brothers in Christ.

"The twelfth chapter of 1 Corinthians describes the Body of Christ, His Church, and its diversity. I believe that when we enter into a cross-cultural relationship, we experience our own uniqueness in that diversity. Our identity becomes more obvious and distinct. That can either become grounds for greater divisiveness or an opportunity for tremendous cross-cultural dialogue. It all depends upon what we intend to do with it. Intentionality!

"Brothers can be different and disagree, but their common heritage, their sense of family, should compel them to deal with one another responsibly and respectfully. That's what I learned as God brought Ray and me together. He enriched my life and that of my family, and I am very thankful."

How to See Diversity

Dan and Ray's story illustrates what two men can do to bridge the cultural barriers to brotherhood. Through Ray's eyes, Dan began to see that men of color have had to work at adapting to the culture that the white middle-class Protestant majority has created. This culture is the constant burden that the man of color must carry every day. He simply doesn't fit! So, Dan humbled himself in prayer and asked God to open his eyes and increase his sensitivity to what Ray faced on a daily basis.

On the other hand, Ray had been raised to believe that the white people held all the money and power. Because they did, he'd been taught that they "held him down." Whether it was true or not didn't matter. It sure seemed to be true. But Ray was also a mature Christian. He knew that it was not that simple. He knew that racism was rooted in the hearts of all men, that it was a question of sin—not skin.

Even though he'd often felt the sting of their "haughty eyes," he knew the Bible said that brotherhood was God's intention. And he acted accordingly. Though he'd often been treated as less than equal, he learned to forgive! He accepted Dan, not as one of "them," but as a potential brother in Christ.

Seeing their responsibilities, Dan and Ray took the following four steps to start the work of trust-building:

◆ They shared their hopes.
◆ They shared their pain and disappointment.
◆ They honored each other's uniqueness.
◆ And, they became each other's advocate.

Share Your Hopes
Dan realized that the member of the dominant culture must take the first step. That is, Dan had to communicate to Ray that he had the same aspirations for his family and community that Ray did. Dan wanted a better life for his children and began to share how he hoped to achieve it. Of course, Ray could identify. But that was only the start.

Even though Ray was capable of great forgivness, he was still carrying the scars of a people that knew the pain of rejection. The pain of feeling locked out of the opportunities America was supposed to offer just because their skin was the wrong color. Ray needed to know that Dan had felt pain, too.

Share Your Pain
So, as their relationship progressed, Dan shared his pain. Dan knew he could not identify with the pain that racial prejudice causes, and he frankly admitted that to Ray. However, Dan had known the deep pain of losing a loved one. In the hopes of deepening their relationship, he shared that with Ray. This vulnerability helped.

Ray saw that Dan knew what it meant to live with pain and the need to press on in spite of it. Together, they discovered that the private scars that men are so hesitant to share are often the passports to each other's heart. No matter what our culture, we've all felt pain and we can all identify with it.

Recognize His Uniqueness

The Bible teaches us to "honor one another," and I didn't see this side of cultural diversity until I heard Ray and Dan's story. Honor means much more than just the politeness of civilized dialogue. Honor means to hold in esteem the other person's uniqueness because you can learn from it. You can grow just because he is in your life and he is who he is. Both Dan and Ray realized that the other man's uniqueness could be used by God to bring them to greater understanding of the meaning of life—and love.

Become His Advocate

As a result, they became one another's advocate. This, too, is part of honoring one another. As time went on and as the value of each other's contribution became more evident, they began to support and defend each other when necessary. However, to get to this point requires time and commitment and, since it is risky, not everyone's ready for it. We fear the unknown, and with greater diversity of backgrounds, there appears to be greater potential for conflict.

However, those who've gone around the bases in the midst of cultural diversity, as Ray and Dan have, can attest to how enriching the experience is. For, as they round third base, diversity isn't just better understood; as these men head for home plate and Christlikeness, diversity is celebrated! And in the process, Christ is glorified in new and exciting ways. Let's let Ray put it in his own words.

> "The thing that first struck me about Dan was his quietness. Although he was obviously an introvert, I could see a sincere desire to reach out to me. It was my first day on the job, and he made me feel as though I belonged. It wasn't till much later that I found out about his extensive ministry among men. Somehow I felt comfortable with him, and eventually we were able to share the pain we had both

encountered in our lives, the pain that made us who we were.

"As we began to share, I discovered that we had many things in common, although initially, I thought we were very different because of our ethnic backgrounds. I found out that his pain, though very different in its origin and nature, was potentially just as devastating to his life as mine had been to me.

"With time our relationship became based on mutual trust. We were sensitive to each other, but also perfectly candid. We discovered that there were many things we could share with each other that were mutually beneficial. Although there are some major differences between us, we have much more in common, such as an honest desire to serve God to the best of our ability, to reach out to men, and to begin to bridge the gap between us. We learned that most of our prejudices were based on ignorance: a lack of knowledge of other people's cultures and history and a lack of will to do anything about it.

"But now, as a result of our relationship and the honor we bestowed on each other, I have a greater sense of personal worth and dignity. This has proven to be a source of strength in time of need. We have gone from being acquaintances, to good friends, and ultimately, to becoming brothers. And I hope that our experience will encourage other men to take the same risks: the risks necessary to break down the walls that divide us—one man at a time."

SUMMARY

We started with an historical example of just how "haughty" one man can be and how ugly that looks to the watching world. But then we saw how difficult it was for an athlete to break into the game of baseball in the United States, just because of his skin color. If we're tempted to think that those days are over, Roger's story painfully reminds us that, fifty years later, the struggle for equality still exists.

To help us face this struggle constructively, therefore, we looked at the process of racial reconciliation through the eyes of two men. We saw the time and effort—intentionality—it takes to cross the historical chasm that separates the minorities from the mainstream in America. We also saw a new beginning, some hope for the long journey toward opening our lives to each other as brothers in Christ.

Just as Dan and Ray learned to share their lives, so can we. We can learn to be comfortable in discussing our hopes and sharing our pain. With more time and effort, we can learn to respect each other's uniquenesses and become each other's advocate. And, as Ray said, Christ can heal our nation through us "one man at a time." In short, on an individual basis, we can catch a glimpse of just how big the Kingdom of God is and how inappropriate our "haughty eyes" can be. As Roger said in his closing challenge, "God help America if we don't!"

DISCUSSION QUESTIONS

1. What did you learn from Jackie Robinson's and Roger's stories?
2. What struck you about Dan's and Ray's cross-cultural experiences?
3. Why do you think the principle of intentionality is so important to the process of reconciliation?
4. Why did Ray conclude with the idea that reconciliation must take place "one man at a time"? In light of history, don't we have to have a more sweeping approach? Why, or why not?

NOTES

Chapter 8
The Equipment Closet: Troubleshooting

Most groups take three steps forward, then two steps back. Problems are an inherent part of the job of leading a group. You can expect plenty of setbacks on your way around the bases. A good player-coach not only needs a game plan but also needs to make mid-game coaching adjustments. The following are some common problems and suggested changes that can be made in your lineup. They were inspired in part by Lyman Coleman's work at the Serendipity House.

1. We seem to be stuck on first base. We're stagnating.

First base is a great place to be, unless some members want to progress further. Then the group will have a problem with differing expectations. We suggested in the first chapter that you go through a period of spring training together. After six to twelve weeks, this provides a natural time of evaluation and recommitment. Ask the group what they really want to do. Though it is possible that they want to stay at the acquaintance level, they can move on with a little prodding by the coach.

2. Our group wants to move around the bases more quickly than the book suggests. Is that possible?

Speed in rounding the bases is possible. It is a product of group desire, honesty, transparency, common commitment, and trust in one another. Often, a crisis will be catalytic in the progress of the group. Don't try to avoid crises. Expect them.

3. How can I tell if we are making progress?

Howard Hendricks says that "the atmosphere you create is more important than the content that you cover." If you, as the group leader, can answer the following questions positively, you are probably right where you need to be.

- ◆ Is caring encouraged? (Have we felt cared for?)
- ◆ Is everyone comfortable with his level of participation?

- Are we comfortable with the level of communication?
- Are we moving at a pace agreeable to all?
- Is there a good balance between the social and the spiritual aspects of the group?
- Is healthy conflict permitted?
- Are the rules of conflict resolution clear in everyone's mind?

4. My group is too diverse. How can I really move the team around the bases with such an assortment of group members?

The following is an overview of the different types of people that may tend to keep a group from progressing, along with some helpful suggestions.

- Some men are very social creatures and have little time for anything else. They're there for the fellowship and will probably not do the work required for the study or the task. A good coach will need to challenge them to go deeper in their walk with God and be willing to pay the price to do so.
- Others feel that they are right. Often they have a holier-than-thou manner which stifles the group. They probably need to remember that Jesus was also very human and communicated in such a way that people were invited into His life.
- Some are very intelligent and they know it. However, Jesus related well to others where they were. A smart person needs to remember that his call to Christ includes his brothers and that he will not experience the love of God without them.
- There are many amateur psychiatrists these days who are giving counsel that is not asked for. These people need to remember that Jesus always asked those who came to Him what He could do for them. If they do the same, they'll stop assuming too much with people.
- Finally, there are those who are just reluctant participants. They'd rather be home watching the game. A gentle challenge in the area of their personal growth should suffice to help them recognize their need for their brothers.

5. One person dominates the discussion.
All group members have a vital contribution to make. It's just a question of clarifying how they should make it and when. This goes back to our listening skills. Members have to be patiently reminded that their agenda is not the only one that's worthy. As obvious as that sounds, people forget it. The leader shouldn't.

6. We seem to disagree about important issues.
There are divisive issues in our Christian culture such as abortion, the use of alcohol, and the role of government. The Scriptures address some of these issues but are silent on others. As a result, throughout its history the Church has tried to adhere to the following motto: "In the essentials, unity. In the nonessentials, diversity. In all things, charity." Where we can, we must let the Bible speak for itself. Otherwise we may be in the area of a nonessential to faith and practice. In that light, here are good reminders when conflict arises:

- ◆ Don't let the talkative people win. Those who need a little more time to formulate their ideas will be uncomfortable with the outcome.
- ◆ Avoid arguing about who's right or who's wrong.
- ◆ Let the Bible speak. Put the focus back on the texts that speak to the issue.
- ◆ Make more observations on those texts.
- ◆ Pray and give the Spirit time to work.

As we said in chapter 3, conflict should be seen as an opportunity to grow in mutual understanding and appreciation of one another.

7. The group is too quiet.
If the members are too quiet: Let them think! The Spirit could be surfacing some issues. After a pause, however, you may want to put the emphasis back upon what they've observed: "What does the text say about this?" If a member is habitually quiet, ask him specifically to share his observations. Remember, good observations must precede interpretations in the discussion of a text or an issue.

85

8. No one seems to want to pray, or our prayers seem superficial.

If prayer seems stifled, there may be a lack of trust in the group. If that is the case, return to first base and plan some activities that will encourage the men to interact in a more informal way. That should rekindle the trust-building and, in time, more prayer should follow. If that doesn't do it, however, plan a study on prayer and begin to keep a journal of prayer requests and answers. Normally, as the men see the answers to their prayers, they will be encouraged to pray. Finally, you might try spending part of a day or weekend praying and fasting.

9. Our sharing time never seems to go very deep.

If the sharing level remains shallow, the leader is probably not setting the example. It's hard to share where we are struggling if the leader is constantly speaking of his victories or those of someone else. It's always easier to talk of "them," "they," or even "we," instead of "I." It's not until we discuss what "I" am going through that the discussion will become more authentic. If that doesn't seem to work, return to first base by planning some informal activities which will allow the group to build more trust.

10. Our time seems to be centered around one person's problems.

If the group is too distracted by a single member's problems, meet with that person individually to determine whether or not he needs to get some help outside the group. Continue the prayer and loving support because any one of us may be dysfunctional for a period of time. Life has a way of happening to us all. However, if the difficulties appear to be prolonged, they are probably beyond the competence of the group and additional outside counseling should be sought.

11. What are some basic expectations we should communicate at the first meeting?

- Attend all meetings whenever possible.
- Read/study any material agreed upon by the group prior to the meeting.
- Be willing to pray at times during the week for group

members.

◆ What goes on in the group will remain appropriately confidential.

◆ We will value the contribution and opinions of each group member and accept him for who he is and where he is.

◆ Everyone is encouraged to participate and share freely, but members are equally free not to participate.

12. What will "bench" the players?
Here are the five basic patterns that men commonly use to put each other back on the bench.

    a. They pacify each other. By that we mean that they are trying to avoid conflict by "not making anyone angry." Honesty is avoided, causing others who are prone to express themselves to be strongly frustrated. These are the "yes men" of life. They always agree. Because of that, some would say that they can't be trusted. They must be challenged to see conflict in a better light and to take some risks with their opinions and ideas.

    b. Some men lack maturity and are always complaining. If the message is constantly negative, even though it may be helpful, it will not be heard. Most people instinctively protect themselves from negative messages. Gripers may be trying to control the situation or improve their status by criticizing others. That hardly leads to acceptance. Remind them of that.

    c. Some men block the process by distracting others. They draw attention to themselves by saying or doing something that has nothing to do with the subject at hand. Their agenda is "me!" They act as if they are not aware that another topic is being discussed. However, like the gripers, until the others learn to ignore them, they can be quite disruptive. Remind them of their obligations to the group's agenda.

    d. Some men are just too calculating. They do not take into account the emotions of the team and the need for morale. They are more logical than even men need to be, and they do not allow themselves to become involved. The messages they send are not clear because they are too self-protective.

This inhibits the sharing and bonding process. Encourage them to take a risk!

e. Finally, some men are just plain prejudiced. They do not know how to suspend judgment and they let their biased feelings speak before the bonding process has really begun. Review the listening skills with them and encourage them to work at accepting others!

13. How do we recognize the players who are so quick to disqualify the others?

Here's just a sample of the moves they use:

a. The *put-down* is normally a sarcastic remark that affects only the person it is aimed at. Often the rest of the group will mistakenly go along with it and chuckle. But the damage is done, and if forgiveness is not sought or given, mutual acceptance will be missed.

b. They *interrupt*, but they don't do it to clarify what the other person is saying. They do it to confront. They jump into the middle of the discussion to refute, not to understand.

c. They *bring up the past* instead of sticking to the topic at hand. This shifts the discussion away from mutual understanding and back to them: their pain, disappointment, and reasons why "it just won't work."

d. They *mind read*! Only they come to the wrong conclusions! Then they state them in such a way that damage is done. It's jumping to conclusions about what people say and why they say it without having the maturity to seek clarification.

e. Finally, they do not watch their *body language*. Their body language is inconsistent with their words. They appear bored. Distracted. Indifferent. They give double messages by saying things in such a way that people can't believe that they mean them. Their tone of voice and gestures just don't match up, and after a while trust is lost.

There are other moves such as *changing the subject*, but these all boil down to one thing: *Their agenda is more important than the group's,* and they will continue to bench the others until they get their way. Eventually they will have to be called

88

on it and reminded that God has something much bigger in mind.

A Challenge!
After all we've covered, if you still want to be involved, then God must be calling you to do it. And if that's the case, let me remind you what the Apostle Paul said: "Be strong in the Lord and in his mighty power. Put on the full armor of God so that you can take your stand against the devil's schemes" (Ephesians 6:10-11).

We must remember that we are in a spiritual struggle and that requires us to take a stand. Nothing less than our own fate, the fate of our children, and the fate of our country is at stake. As we enter into the arena of spiritual warfare, however, we must expect to be attacked and, on occasion, suffer some setbacks. There will be losses. Some will quit.

But it's my firm conviction that the men who will have a positive spiritual impact upon this country are those who've learned to stand back to back, shoulder to shoulder as brothers. Men who've learned to discard the petty differences that divide them in light of the great calling that unites them.

SUMMARY
We've seen that an essential ingredient of a successful small group is a player-coach, a leader who's been around the bases before. But even with that, in the normal life span of a group, there is a stormy readjustment of expectations and communication patterns. Again, this is normal, and we must always expect that there will be clashes of temperament and personality.

However, these should not discourage us. Remember, people are coming to get their needs met, so an honest, open dialogue with the group or its individual members should resolve difficulties if they are approached in prayer and humility. Of course, in these areas, the leader should be the example.

For more on trouble-shooting, see *How to Lead Small Groups* by Neal McBride (NavPress).

DISCUSSION QUESTIONS
1. Have you ever been in a situation where the group seemed to be stagnating or disbanding prematurely? Explain.

2. Knowing now what's in the equipment closet, what would you have done differently?
3. Are any of the other items in the above troubleshooting list relevant to your group right now? If so, which ones?
4. Read Ephesians 6:10-18 and discuss the implications of spiritual warfare for your group.

NOTES

Appendix 1
"One Another"
Bible Study

When the group senses that it is ready, the following study may be helpful to begin to investigate the Scriptures together. Jesus told His followers in John 13:34-35, "As I have loved you, so you must love one another. By this all men will know that you are my disciples, if you love one another." Love is the mark of the brothers. Often "love" seems nebulous. But as invisible light when directed through a prism produces distinct colors and hues, so too the practical expression of love has been clearly defined in the "one another" verses of the Bible.

I. **Select a "One Another" Verse:** Why do you want to study this verse?

II. **Observe the Passage by Asking Questions:** Think through the significance of your answers.

Who is speaking or writing and to whom?

What is the passage about?

Why does the author/speaker say/write about what he does?

How does this passage fit into the context?

How would you define each of the key words in this passage?

What insight or illustrations do cross-references give you?

What are the effects or benefits of obeying this command?

What is the opposite of this command?

What are the effects of practicing the opposite?

How is this action similar/different in the lives of the Christians you know?

III. **What Is the "Natural Question" That Arises From the Passage?** The natural question has to do with "So what? How does this apply to me?" It will usually be "How can I . . . ?" "Why should I . . . ?" or "What does it mean to . . . ?" You may have to experiment with several types of questions until you find the right one.

IV. **Answer the "Natural Question" From the Passage Being Studied:** On a separate page, put your answer in the form of an outline. These answers are really *principles* of life and ministry. With each principle (each point in your outline), you will want to *explain it* (interpretation), *illustrate it* (from the Bible and personal experience of how this principle worked out both positively and/or negatively), and *apply it*. Every point in your outline may not have a specific application.

V. **Application:** What are the possible applications of this passage in relation to:

Your spiritual leaders?

Your colleagues?

Your children?

Your spouse?

Your friends?

What are your barriers to application? What will this cost you?

What will you do today to apply what you have learned?

Who will you share your discoveries with?

"ONE ANOTHER" VERSES
(a partial list)

Love one another.
John 13:34-35, Galatians 5:14
Encourage one another.
Hebrews 3:13, Hebrews 10:24-25, 1 Thessalonians 5:11

Be devoted to one another.
Romans 12:10
Give preference to one another.
Romans 12:10
Build up one another.
Romans 14:19, 1 Thessalonians 5:11
Be kind to one another.
1 Thessalonians 5:15
Live in harmony with one another.
Romans 12:16
Accept one another.
Romans 15:7
Serve one another.
Galatians 5:13
Submit to one another.
Ephesians 5:21
Have concern for one another.
1 Corinthians 12:25
Be kind, compassionate . . . forgiving each other.
Ephesians 4:32
Carry each other's burdens.
Galatians 6:2
Teach and admonish one another.
Colossians 3:16
Confess your sins to one another.
James 5:16
Pray for one another.
James 5:16
Offer hospitality to one another.
1 Peter 4:9
Don't judge one another.
Romans 14:13
Don't slander one another.
James 4:11
Don't provoke one another.
Galatians 5:26

You may want to start by studying "love one another," "accept one another," and "forgive one another," since these are all given in relationship to how Christ has loved, accepted, and forgiven us.

Appendix 2

Accountability Questions for Men's Small Groups

When the group senses that it is ready, the following list of questions may serve as a guide for deepening the relational patterns and helping each other keep their promises. They come from, *Focusing Your Men's Ministry*, by Pete Richardson.

1. How much time did you spend in prayer this week?
2. Did you pray for others in this group?
3. Did you put yourself in an awkward situation with a woman?
4. At any time did you compromise your integrity?
5. What one sin plagued your walk with God this week?
6. Did you accomplish your spiritual goals this week?
7. Are you giving to the Lord's work financially?
8. How have you demonstrated a servant's heart?
9. Do you treat your peers and coworkers as people loved by God?
10. What significant thing did you do for your wife and/or family?
11. What was your biggest disappointment? How did you decide to handle it?
12. What was your biggest joy? Did you thank God?
13. What do you see as your number one need for next week?
14. Are you satisfied with the time you spent with the Lord this week?
15. Did you take time to show compassion for others in need?
16. Did you control your tongue?
17. What did you do this week to enhance your relationship with your spouse?
18. Did you pray and read God's Word this week? What did you derive from this time?
19. In what ways have you launched out in faith since we last met?
20. In what ways has God blessed you this week? And what disappointments consumed your thoughts this week?
21. Did you look at a woman in the wrong way?
22. How have you been tempted this week? How did you respond?

23. How has your relationship with Christ been changing?
24. Did you worship in church this week?
25. Have you shared your faith this week? How?
26. What are you wrestling with in your thought life?
27. What have you done for someone else this week?
28. Are the "visible" you and the "real" you consistent in this relationship?

Remember, these questions are offered only as a guide, not as a standard, and should not be used until the group is ready for them.

Read 2 Samuel 11–12 and make observations about the life of David and the need we all have to be accountable to one another. Make your observations below:

Appendix 3

The Joy of DSI:
Discovery, Sharing, and Interceding

(Provided as a possible method for small-group Bible study.)

PART I

The "W Questions"—Who? What? When? Where? Why? (and also How?)—are an investigative reporter's "best friends." They are useful in all phases of investigative Bible study, especially in *observation* or fact-finding, in which you read and research.

Then ask more "W Questions"—Why? So *what*?—to get at the meaning or significance of the passage during the *interpretation* phase of Bible study.

Use more "W Questions"—Which one has my name on it? Why me? Now *what*?—to aid you in generalizing and personalizing the biblical truth to your life situation. This third phase is called *application*.

With the "W Questions" as your digging tools, dig into Philippians 2:19-30.

OBSERVATION

1. Who is talking here? Who are the characters named, addressed, or alluded to in this passage?

2. What distinguishes Timothy and Epaphroditus from "everyone else"? Or how are they different than "everyone else"? *That question can be broken into three parts:*

   a. What defines "everyone"? (verses 20-21)
   b. What defines Timothy? How is he described? (verses 19-23)
   c. What defines Epaphroditus? How is he different? (verses 25-30)

3. In the context of the rest of Philippians 2, what are the interests of Jesus Christ? (verse 21)

4. Why is Paul commending these men to the Philippians? Why would Paul (or any other leader of a men's ministry) want to build a team around such men?

5. If you were to be like Timothy (and not like "everyone else") as a "son to a father," who stands out as your "Paul," the person from whom you have learned so much or under whom you now minister? How will you pray for that person today?

6. If you were to be like Epaphroditus (and not "everyone else"), who are the brothers in the Lord's work with whom you labor side by side from week to week?

7. If you were to be like Paul, who are the ones you have fathered or mentored in the faith? That is, who do you feel responsible for, whom you will minister to this next week? How will you pray for them?

8. Ministry involves a people focus that welcomes another man in the Lord with joy and honors men like Timothy and Epaphroditus (2:29). How can you show such welcome and honor to the men in your circle of influence when you get home?

PART II

If you really were Timothy, Epaphroditus, Paul, or "everyone else" in the previous study (see Part I), you would have certain concerns or special interests that characterize your life at this particular juncture in your life and ministry. You would be praying for your "sons" in the faith, your "fathers" in the Lord, your "brothers" in the ministry, your concerns for someone's health, your church's welfare, advancement of the interests of Christ in the community, etc.

With their example and your own present life situation to reflect upon, share in small groups (1) a personal relationship (troubling or healthy) or (2) a specific event (past, present, or future) for their prayer support. Each time someone names a specific prayer concern, the person to his right prays for that concern until you share-and-intercede your way around the group.

The space that follows is for taking notes, which you would do if you were making a covenant to pray for these men during the week, from now until you meet again, or until there is an answer one way or another to the prayer.

NAME	PRAYER REQUEST	ANSWER TO PRAYER
1.		
2.		
3.		
4.		
5.		

This DSI material comes from Chuck Miller's ministry Barnabas, Inc., Lake Forest, California.

Read Psalm 119 in its entirety and make a partial list below of all the benefits that come to the man who masters God's Word.

1.

2.

3.

4.

5.

6.

7.

8.

9.

10.

Read Psalm 1 and discuss the prerequisites of a godly man.

1.

2.

3.

4.

Appendix 4
Confusion and Isolation in the American Male

(Provided to stimulate small-group discussion.)

Results! That's what counts in a global economy driven by the bottom line and the speed of computer technology. What this competition will do to the American male's ability to relate to his peers in a meaningful way remains to be seen. But if the past is any indication, men will probably be more driven by stress than led by God.

The White Collar Man
In his book *Ordering Your Private World*, Gordon McDonald presents what he has discovered to be symptomatic of a "driven man":

- He's results-oriented.
- He's in constant pursuit of expansion.
- He's restless and very intense.
- He's very competitive.
- His people skills are underdeveloped.
- He's "too busy for integrity."
- He's preoccupied with the symbols of achievement.

But what are those symbols of achievement? What he does, what he owns, and who he knows! In the process, who he really is gets crushed in the rush for more, bigger, and better.

The Blue Collar Man
What does economic pressure do to the working man who shoulders the tax burden, pays the rising medical costs, and must make do with a shrinking paycheck? Since he's not a policy maker, he often feels powerless to influence his own destiny. Therefore, he frequently questions his place among other men. He feels insecure because at any moment he could be discarded by a driven manager or replaced by a machine.

The Androgynous Man

The feminism of the sixties and seventies has done much to raise the awareness of the plight of women around the world and should be applauded for doing so. However, it has also raised a debate in the American consciousness about the nature of sexuality which will continue on well into the nineties. As a result of this debate, Dr. Rod Cooper, a professor at Denver Seminary, feels that the modern American male is caught in a series of "double-binds" with respect to his masculinity.

For example, if a man shows his feelings, he's considered by some to be "neurotic and unstable." But if he represses them, others would say that he's "aloof and uncaring." If he spends time with the family, some would say he doesn't care about his work; but if he spends too much time at work, some would say he's neglecting the family. The debate goes on until a man is criticized for seeking a promotion and thought to be rather mediocre if he · doesn't. So, what's a man to do?

The "Strong, Silent Type"

Is a man supposed to embody the all-American male mystique? You've seen him on the screen. He's the pioneer who's opening up the west or the rogue cop who's cleaning up the city. He doesn't say much—he acts. He doesn't smile—he grunts. He does not reveal much—he controls. And he never stays anywhere very long—he's always on the move. And though these characters portrayed by men such as John Wayne, Clint Eastwood, Steve McQueen, and others did well at the box office, weren't they also relationally bankrupt?

Isolation

The above images of manhood can cause some confusion. When they are intensified by a period of pain, they can lead a man to withdraw from family, friends, and society. If this pattern of withdrawal continues, a man may find himself feeling isolated and not really know why. Isolation stems from that prolonged self-imposed withdrawal that is characteristic of most men when they're under stress. This leads to friendlessness and a profound sense of alienation from oneself, others, and purpose in life. If a brother and the grace of God do not intervene in this withdrawal process, a man may pass through increasingly painful phases of isolation:

burnout, depression, and finally, *wounding.*

Burnout: This phase is characterized by increasing fatigue and a lack of motivation for the normal routines of life. Normally, at this point, a brother can suggest a long-needed vacation or sabbatical, and with some rest and a little recreation ("R and R"), a man can normally bounce back.

Depression: If burnout is not recognized soon enough, however, a man can pass unknowingly into a depression. Though some temperaments are more prone to depression than others, most men will likely experience some sort of aggravated burnout or depression in their life.

The symptoms are again fatigue and lack of motivation for the job and family. However, in this phase, a lack of motivation for life itself also begins to creep into the mind. There's an overwhelming sense of "what's the use?" As the meaning of life becomes more vague, despair sets in. Without the help of some brothers at this point, a man can fall into the final and most deeply painful experience of isolation.

Wounding: This phase is characterized by feelings of betrayal. Betrayal by a wife, a friend, or a business partner can cut the legs out from under a man and leave him with a sense of falling, with no one to catch him—not even God!

Feeling betrayed by others, whoever they may be, also leads to a sense of feeling self-betrayed—"How could I have been so stupid?" If that is not checked with the love of a brother who has been there, then the man will eventually feel betrayed by God Himself—"How could He have let this happen to me? After all, isn't He supposed to be loving?"

Of course God is loving! But His method is men. There is only one cure for this depth of isolation——a lot of time, patience, and understanding by some brothers. The wounded man is most helped by a brother's prayers and silent attention to his physical and psychological needs. Who else but a brother would do that?

DISCUSSION QUESTIONS

1. What did you think of the cultural obstacles described above? Did you identify with any of the above descriptions?
2. Do you think that the process of self-isolation described above is universal among men? Why, or why not?

3. Have you ever experienced a period of isolation in your life? Would you care to describe it to the team?
4. What did it take to break out of your isolation? How were you helped?

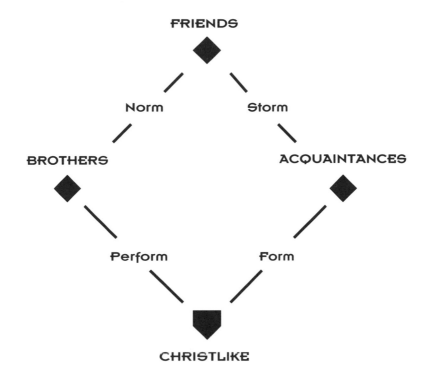

While Dr. Glenn Wagner was doing his graduate work, he took a course on leadership and leadership development. He suggested to me that its basic thesis could be used as an alternative way of looking at the relational diamond, and I agree. So we offer this brief discussion of the "baselines" to more fully develop the model.

Just as there are the four baselines to a baseball diamond, there are four developmental phases in the life of a small group of men: *form, storm, norm,* and *perform.*

Form is the baseline that leads to first base and the mutual acceptance of one another. Form is what is determined by the purpose and the parameters of the group: open or closed, affinity or diversity, and what elements of support, study, or task the group will emphasize.

After the form comes the *storm!* That is, for reasons which we've discussed previously, there will have to be some adjustment of expectations and styles to accommodate the group if it is to progress to second base in genuine friendship. The men will have to have a few fair fights in order to ensure a certain level of honesty and respect.

After they've done that, however, there is a new *norm* that is established as they approach third base. Its foundation is the mutual respect and complementary perspectives that have emerged during the storm. At this point the men can begin to learn from each others' strengths and can begin the processes leading to covenants and accountability to one another. They're brothers.

As they head for home plate and the Christlikeness that represents, they begin to benefit from the teamwork they've developed and can now *perform* as men who are accountable to each other. The dynamic of the Body of Christ can be felt as the men not only minister to each other but begin to influence their respective communities as well. This is what it means to perform as men of integrity, men who are growing in Christlikeness.

So what are we waiting for? Let's play ball!

NOTES

106

Appendix 6
More on Listening Skills

There are four attitudes that characterize good listening skills. First, we must learn to give the other person's ideas priority in our thinking. Therefore, *suspend our agenda!* Our questions should be aimed at drawing him out further, not in steering the discussion toward us. A simple, "Tell me more about that" usually suffices to draw a man out and communicates to him that we value his observations.

Second, our goal is acceptance. Therefore, *suspend judgment.* Give him the benefit of the doubt. We don't need to disagree right away. There will be plenty of time for that later. Right now, what we want to accomplish is to understand as much as possible where this other fellow is coming from. So, let's hear a few more, "Tell me mores. . . ." Listening, more than anything else, will communicate that you accept him.

Third, try to paraphrase what you've just heard. Give the other person some *feedback* to make sure that you understand. "Now, let me see if I have you right, George. You said that . . . is that right?" This will communicate that you value his contribution.

Fourth, *remember* that this is a Divine encounter. God Himself is involved in this dynamic. A difference of opinion, therefore, is not really grounds for ending the relationship or walking off in a huff. This man is not your enemy, he's your brother, and a representative of the Body of Christ. Remember that and treat him accordingly.

The following are twenty statements that describe behaviors a person usually finds irritating because he feels he is not being listened to:

1. The other person doesn't give me a chance to talk. I go in with a problem and never get a chance to tell about it.
2. The other person interrupts me when I talk.
3. The other person never looks at me when I talk. I don't know whether he is listening or not.

4. The other person continually fidgets with a pencil, a paper, or something, looking at it and examining it rather than listening to me.
5. The other person treats me like an inferior.
6. The other person never smiles—I'm afraid to talk to him.
7. The other person asks questions as if he doubts everything I say.
8. Whenever I make a suggestion, the other person always throws cold water on me.
9. The other person is always trying to get ahead of my story and guess what my point is, sometimes even finishing my sentence for me.
10. The other person frequently answers a question with another question, and usually I can't answer. It embarrasses me.
11. The other person argues with everything I say—even before I have a chance to finish stating my case.
12. Everything I say reminds the other person of an experience he has had or a happening he has heard of recently. I get frustrated when he continually interrupts to say, "That reminds me. . . ."
13. The other person sits there picking hangnails, or clipping fingernails, or cleaning his glasses, etc. I know he can't do that and listen, too.
14. He just waits for me to get through talking so he can interject something of his own.
15. When I have a good idea, he takes credit for it by saying something like, "Oh, yes, I have been thinking about that, too."
16. The other person stares at me when I'm talking and looks me in the eye so directly that I feel self-conscious.
17. The other person overdoes being attentive—too many nods of his head, or mm-mms or uh-huhs.
18. The other person inserts humorous remarks when I am trying to be serious.
19. The other person acts as if he is doing me a favor in seeing me, and frequently looks at the clock or his watch while I am talking.
20. The other person passes the buck about problems I raise.

Bibliography

Coleman, Lyman. *Beginning a Men's Group.* Littleton, CO: Serendipity House, 1991.

Hicks, Robert. *The Masculine Journey.* Colorado Springs, CO: NavPress, 1993.

Hicks, Robert. *Uneasy Manhood.* Nashville, TN: Oliver-Nelson, 1992.

Kouzes, James M., and Posner, Barry Z. *The Leadership Challange.* San Fransisco, CA: Jossy-Bass Publishers, 1987.

MacDonald, Gordon. *Ordering Your Private World.* Nashville, TN: Thomas Nelson, 1986.

Morely, Pat. *The Man in the Mirror.* Brentwood, TN: Wolgemuth and Hyatt, 1989.

Rainey, Dennis. *The Home Builders Study Guide.* Orlando, FL: Word Publications, 1989.

Richardson, Pete. *Focusing Your Men's Ministry.* Boulder, CO: Promise Keepers, 1993.

SMALL-GROUP MATERIALS FROM NAVPRESS

BIBLE STUDY SERIES

DESIGN FOR DISCIPLESHIP
GOD IN YOU
GOD'S DESIGN FOR THE FAMILY
INSTITUTE OF BIBLICAL
  COUNSELING SERIES

LEARNING TO LOVE SERIES
LIFECHANGE
LOVE ONE ANOTHER
STUDIES IN CHRISTIAN LIVING
THINKING THROUGH DISCIPLESHIP

TOPICAL BIBLE STUDIES

Becoming a Woman of
  Excellence
Becoming a Woman of Freedom
Becoming a Woman of Purpose
The Blessing Study Guide
Celebrating Life
Growing in Christ
Growing Strong in God's Family
Homemaking
Intimacy with God

Loving Your Husband
Loving Your Wife
A Mother's Legacy
Strategies for a Successful
  Marriage
Surviving Life in the Fast Lane
To Run and Not Grow Tired
To Walk and Not Grow Weary
What God Does When Men Pray
When the Squeeze Is On

BIBLE STUDIES WITH COMPANION BOOKS

Bold Love
The Feminine Journey
From Bondage to Bonding
Hiding from Love
Inside Out
The Masculine Journey
The Practice of Godliness
The Pursuit of Holiness

Secret Longings of the
  Heart
Spiritual Disciplines
Tame Your Fears
Transforming Grace
Trusting God
What Makes a Man?
The Wounded Heart
Your Work Matters to God

RESOURCES

Brothers!
How to Lead Small Groups
Jesus Cares for Women
The Small Group Leaders
  Training Course

Topical Memory System (KJV/NIV
  and NASB/NKJV)
Topical Memory System: Life
  Issues (KJV/NIV and
  NASB/NKJV)

VIDEO PACKAGES

Bold Love
Hope Has Its Reasons
Inside Out
Living Proof

Parenting Adolescents
Unlocking Your Sixth Suitcase
Your Home, A Lighthouse